T

District

40 favourite Walks

published by
pocket mountains ltd
The Old Church, Annanside,
Moffat DG10 9HB

ISBN: 978-1-907025-778

Text and photography copyright © Ben Giles 2021

A catalogue record for this book is available from the British Library

Contains Ordnance Survey data © Crown copyright and database 2021 supported by out of copyright mapping 1945-1961

Printed by J Thomson Colour Printers, Glasgow

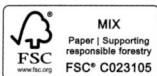

FSC
www.fsc.org

MIX
Paper | Supporting
responsible forestry
FSC® C023105

Introduction

The Peak District still offers its share of wonders, though whether Thomas Hobbes and Daniel Defoe, amongst others, were right to limit the number to seven is a moot point. You only have to set off on foot to give yourself the chance of finding other likely candidates. The Peak forms the southern outcrop of the Pennines and this region of *peacs*, Old English for hill, and high moorland lies at the very heart of England. Looking out from its highest point on Kinder Plateau towards the horizon it is salutary to note that more than 15 million people live within a couple of hours' journey in the encircling ring of cities. Close by to the east sits Sheffield, with Nottingham, Derby and Stoke-on-Trent to the south. To the west, beyond Stockport, is the great city of Manchester, while Bradford and Leeds are more distant over the horizon to the north. Add to this an inner ring of towns crowding in – Glossop, Huddersfield, Barnsley, Chesterfield, Matlock, Ashbourne, Leek, Congleton, Macclesfield – while the market towns of Buxton and Bakewell occupy the centre. Yet people still come, more than ten million each year, to seek out what cities cannot provide.

Traditionally the Peak District is split into two areas, the Dark and White Peak. The Dark Peak's high gritstone moorlands and broad shale valleys are found to the north of the region, notably on the Bleaklow and Kinder plateaus, to the east above the valley of the River Derwent and to the west in a line of high moorland extending southwestwards along Axe Edge, a watershed of five rivers, towards the town of Leek. Enclosed on these three sides is the lighter limestone rock of the White Peak. Castleton and the Hope Valley mark its visible northern boundary and its best known features are the rolling farmland and steep-sided valleys, called dales, around and above the Rivers Manifold, Dove and Wye.

In the Dark Peak are found many of the region's reservoirs, shale being impermeable to water, while the moorlands are covered by a thick layer of peat. Having its own kind of rugged beauty, especially when the heather, bilberry and cottongrass colour the landscape, it also forms the notorious peat hags and mosses, or bogs, which can reduce the unwary walker, intent on covering a certain distance in a certain time, to depths of even greater despair. More carefree wandering is provided by the limestone hills, plateau and dales of the White Peak. Deposited 350 million years ago, when the region lay under an equatorial tropical sea, the limestone is some 20 million years older than the surrounding gritstone. People are drawn equally by the dry-walled uplands as by the ancient, flower-rich woodlands and riversides in the dales and gorges.

The Peak District is also famous for becoming England's first national park.

It was created in 1951 and covers an area of 1438 square kilometres (555 square miles). Almost 40,000 people live within the Peak District National Park, whose limits are marked by millstones, symbolic of the region's industrial past. Its boundary was the subject of much debate and compromise, one of the largest anomalies being the exclusion of the town of Buxton on its western border. The vast majority of the land within the national park is privately owned. Indeed, private land-ownership was one of the major obstacles to its formation.

During the first decades of the 20th century tensions arose between wealthy private landowners, concerned for their shooting and farming rights, and people escaping the surrounding industrialised cities for green spaces and fresher air. By the 1930s there were angry exchanges between gamekeepers and ramblers, who arrived in their hundreds, even thousands, by weekend trains from Manchester and Sheffield in particular. The most notorious confrontation has become known as the Kinder Mass Trespass, when, on 24 April 1932, about five hundred people headed up Kinder Scout via William Clough in an attempt to assert their right to walk over the moorland. In the ensuing scuffles, five protesters were arrested and subsequently imprisoned. It took almost another 20 years for the National Parks and Access to the Countryside Act 1949 to be passed and

a further 50 years' wait for the Countryside and Rights of Way Act 2000 to establish new rights of access to open country throughout England and Wales. As a result of this Act, there are now 524 square kilometres (202 square miles) of open Access Land in the Peak District National Park.

About this guide

This guide contains 40 circular routes in and around the Peak District National Park, ranging in length from 2km to 22km. Many of the routes are intended as comfortable walks or strolls, at most requiring half a day to complete, though a good number can be covered in an hour or two. Some of the routes are longer and on exposed or steep terrain. Here greater exertion, fitness and adequate hill-walking skills will be needed. However, in general the walking is on well-worn paths, lanes and tracks, with plenty of waymarks to help with route-finding.

The route descriptions concentrate on the salient points of navigation and highlight the major twists and turns. If in doubt, the obvious path is usually the line to take. In addition, the accompanying sketch maps serve an illustrative purpose. For the more remote or higher hill routes a map, and on a few routes a compass, should be carried. The relevant OS maps are: Peak District (Dark Peak) Explorer OL1, Peak District (White Peak) Explorer OL24 and Derby Explorer 259. The recommended time for each walk is an estimate based on an average walking speed of 4kmph, with an allowance added in for ascent and type of terrain. However, this will vary significantly, not only for individuals but also given the seasonal effects on paths, especially those on moorlands.

Getting around & access

All the main cities and most of the towns in and around the Peak District have regular bus or train services. An effort has been made to start walks from places which are served by public transport and it would usually be possible, especially in summer months, to plan the completion of a walk to coincide with bus and train times. However, many outlying areas in the Peak District are only intermittently served by public bus on both a weekly and seasonal basis. Access by car is the preferred option for many and, while towns cater adequately for parking, in high season car parks and roadside bays can be completely full. In addition, parking is a sensitive issue in small villages and hamlets. Pubs and inns can be very accommodating if the intention is to visit before or after a walk, but where parking is away from designated car parks consideration should be shown for the needs and access of local residents and, in particular, for farm vehicles.

More than 80% of the national park is designated as farmland and there are more than 2000 farms. Most land is either permanent grass or rough grazing, supporting about 85,000 cattle and more than 400,000 sheep. Especially at lambing and calving time, farmers regularly post notices requesting that dogs are kept on leads. The presence of dogs with calves can be problematic and it is not unheard of for cattle to behave in a very protective way. Even without a dog, cows which have recently calved should be left well alone. If in doubt, it is usually possible to find a short detour to avoid such livestock.

Most paths covered in the routes are well maintained by the Peak District National Park Authority and other local agencies, but in spring and summer some routes can become overgrown and certain paths, especially in winter, are subject to flooding, even quite some time after periods of rain. Higher routes are subject to severely restricted visibility in poor weather and the cloud level can descend very quickly to cover moors and hills. Snow is common on the higher ground in winter months, which can not only make walking routes a more strenuous undertaking but can also affect access by road. Since 2000 the Countryside and Rights of Way Act has opened up legal access to large areas of uplands and moorland. Ordnance Survey maps mark the limit of Access Land, where open country is shaded in yellow, while on the ground look out for the circular brown discs with the symbol of a walker against a white background.

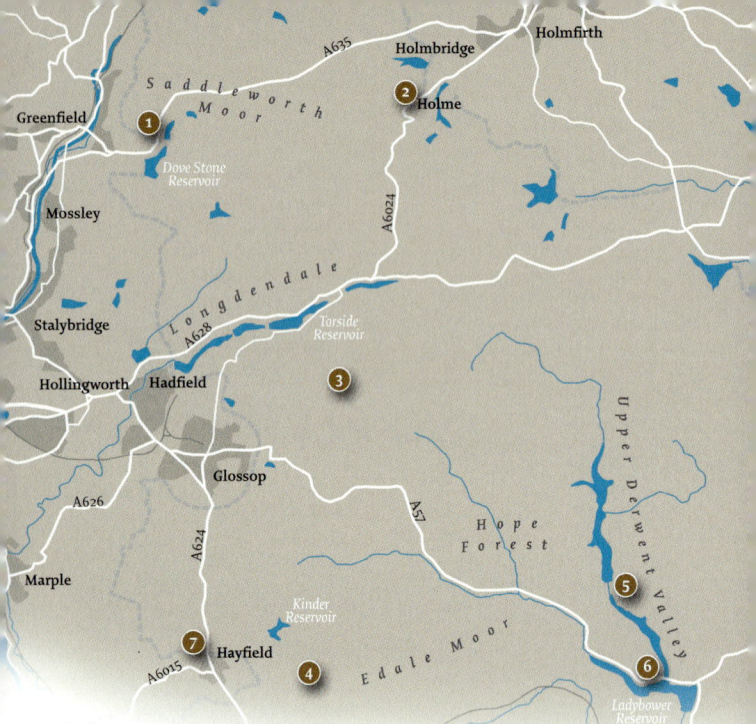

The former cotton town of Glossop lies just outside the national park but right on the fringe of the high moorland which characterises the northern limits of the Peak District. Three valleys with routes over the high passes of the Dark Peak cut across the gritstone uplands from Manchester in the west to Sheffield in the east. Longdendale separates Saddleworth Moor and a series of high reservoirs from the plateau of Bleaklow to its south. The Old English *blaec hlaw* aptly describes this 'dark-coloured hill'. Its remoteness and the need for a long approach, as well as its expanses of peat hags and mosses, can deter walkers but the sense of solitude has its own rewards. Its neighbour to the south across the Snake Pass is more popular. Lying at the southern end of the Pennines and stretching to the Vale of Edale, Kinder Scout is possibly the best known area of peat and heather in the country. Further to the east lie the headwaters of the mighty Derwent, its reservoirs and a series of west-facing edges, topped with weathered tors.

On Derwent Edge looking north to Lost Lad ▶

Glossop and the North

Alderman's Hill

Distance 6km **Time** 2 hours 30
Terrain paths and tracks; rough grassy
hillside with some steep ascent
Map OS Explorer OL1 **Access** bus from
Holmfirth stops at junction of A635 with
Bank Lane

**A short but tough route with one lung-
busting ascent, but the rewards are that
you can avoid the crowds around the
reservoir and gain some stunning views
over Saddleworth Moor.**

Dove Stone Reservoir can be very
popular on summer weekends. Walkers,
joggers, cyclists, climbers and sailors all
come here to enjoy this western edge of
the national park just a short distance
from Manchester. Dove Stone, built in the
1960s, is the youngest of the four
reservoirs in the Greenfield and Chew
Valleys. Many people stick to the waterside
paths or make for Chew Reservoir, but this
route heads for the impressive outcrop of
Alderman's Hill to the north.

The walk starts from Dove Stone
Reservoir car park off the A635, 1.5km east
of Greenfield. With the top of Alderman's
Hill straight ahead, walk across the
reservoir's dam to its north side. Zigzag
up the walkway ahead and then bear left
off the reservoir-side path up the grassy
bank to a gate, where you should bear
right up along the edge of a plantation to
a second gate. In another 100m at a fork in
the path keep left uphill, across a lane,
and up to Binn Green car park.

Across the A635 turn left through a gate
onto the footpath and in 20m head over
the stile in the fence on the right and
continue over the shoulder of the hill to a
wall. Here, ready yourself for 150m of
ascent as the path bears right with the
wall, steeply uphill. Where the wall turns
left across the slope keep ahead uphill

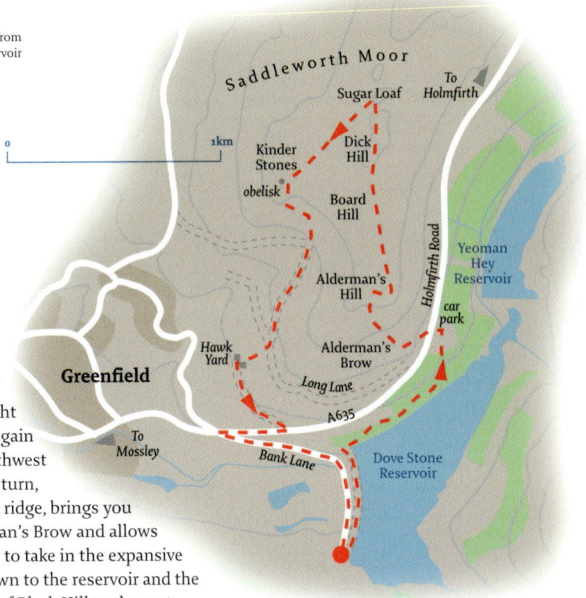

◀ Alderman's Hill from
Dove Stone Reservoir

just to the right of the crag to gain the hill's southwest ridge. A right turn, following the ridge, brings you up to Alderman's Brow and allows for a breather to take in the expansive view back down to the reservoir and the high ground of Black Hill to the east.

The highest point of the hill lies 650m to the north. Take the right-hand of two paths and head over the top of the rise and down to a track junction, from which you can detour out and back to the northerly tops and some great views on a clear day over Saddleworth Moor to the Pennine Hills.

From the junction the route heads westwards down the track across a small dip to reach the obvious obelisk, a war memorial to the men of Saddleworth and Springhead. To continue, take care to head south from the obelisk to the small crag, where a footpath twists its way southeastwards downhill to a gate and a cross-paths. Keep heading down, now SSW, for 450m, initially between tumble-down walls, to a second cross-paths.

Here, walk on down the field beyond to the cottages of Hawk Yard and then turn left along the track for 400m to reach the A635. A right turn along the pavement for 300m brings you opposite the junction of Bank Lane. Cross the road and follow this lane back to the dam and the start.

Black Hill

Distance 11.5km **Time** 4 hours
Terrain lanes, fields and moorland, with
450m of ascent **Map** OS Explorer OL1
Access bus to Holme from Huddersfield
and Glossop

**A walk of contrasts from the delightful
village of Holme, with the option to
climb to the high point of Black Hill on
an out-and-back detour.**

The village of Holme lies 4km
southwest of the well-known town of
Holmfirth, while to the south lies Holme
Moss Transmitting Station, famous for
being the highest of its kind in England.
Near the end of the walk the route passes
over Bilberry Reservoir.

This place has a somewhat grim history.
The original construction of the dam in
the 1840s was rushed through, with
disastrous results. On a February night in
1852 the new under-funded dam

collapsed. It caused massive destruction
in the Digley Valley and at Holmfirth, and
resulted in the deaths of over 80 people.
Nowadays, it's a scenic and tranquil spot.

From the cobbled square in the centre
of the village of Holme, just along from
The Fleece Inn, head up Meal Hill Road,
past the village play area and then the
school before bending right up past Meal
Hill Farm. Beyond, ignore the rough lane
off right and stay on the road as it bends
left and becomes the track of Issues Road,
though some locals use the name Stoney
Lane. With a sense of wide open space and
long views the track bears WSW for the
next 1.2km between improved fields,
down across a dip and up to a gate onto
the open moorland. Keep ahead for 400m
to a point where the path forks.

The route out and back to Black Hill
takes the left fork on the moorland path
ahead, which in 200m crosses a stream

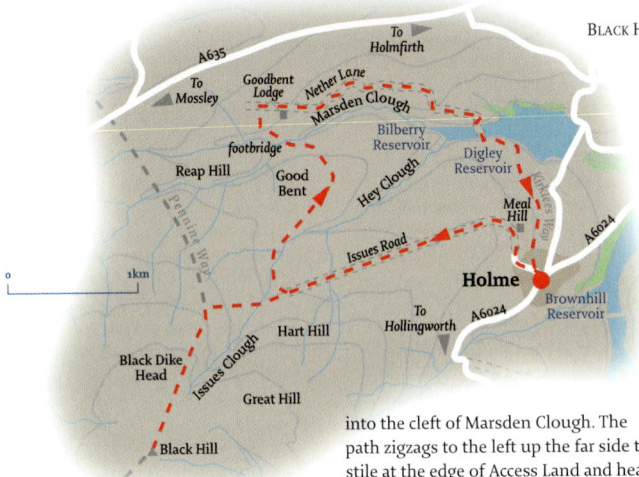

and then climbs the slope on the far side. Carry straight on up the slope beside the grough (ditch) through the bilberry, bracken and heather, at times wet and rough going, to reach the junction with the Pennine Way. A left turn past a small cairn up the trail's stone slabs leads to the top of the rise, beyond which cairns mark the way to the summit triangulation point. The Ordnance Survey map records the name of Soldier's Lump, a possible reference to the military engineers who originally laboured up here in the 18th century with their equipment to survey this remote moorland. Now the stone slabs of the Pennine Way make for easier going, but any deviation might still have you knee-deep in the peat. Return the same way.

To continue from the path-fork, head northwards (SP Footpath) across Issues Clough and over the shoulder of the rise ahead before veering left and descending into the cleft of Marsden Clough. The path zigzags to the left up the far side to a stile at the edge of Access Land and heads up the field beyond to the junction with the track of Nether Lane and the route of the Kirklees Way, which is now followed for the rest of the walk.

Turn right along Nether Lane, past Goodbent Lodge, as it twists its way gently down. After 1km you pass two stone barns and, in another 150m, take care to turn right at the track junction to stay on the Kirklees Way. This soon bears left above Bilberry Reservoir and, after another 350m, zigzags its way down to the walkway between the reservoirs of Bilberry and Digley.

On the far side bear left up alongside a fence and pass through two gates. After the second gate, ignore the track off to the left and keep on the Kirklees Way as it bears half-right up the grassy bank ahead and over a series of eight fields, clearly waymarked, to arrive at a walled walkway. This leads back to Meal Hill Road just up from the centre of the village.

◀ Cottongrass on Black Hill

Bleaklow

Distance 22km **Time** 6 hours 30
Terrain lanes, fields, rocky paths and
exposed moorland, with ascent of 700m
Map OS Explorer OL1 **Access** train (to
Hadfield) from Manchester and bus
from Glossop

One of the classic Peak District routes
over the high Bleaklow plateau. Much
of this walk is over high and remote
moorland and a map and compass
should be taken.

The walk starts from the car park just
beyond Hadfield Station at the end of the
Longdendale Trail (GR025961). Pass under
the railway bridge and keep left along
Platt Street, which soon bears right uphill
for 500m to a right-hand bend. Here, turn
left onto a footpath to Little Padfield
Farm. Beyond the farm buildings a right
turn takes you into a series of fields –
branch right across a stream into the third

field and after passing a cemetery bear left
up to Woodhead Road.

A dogleg right for 30m, then left leads
you down over fields to Swineshaw
Reservoir and below it into woodland to a
lane. Turn right past a small reservoir and
in 250m keep ahead on the footpath down
past the filter station and under the
squared arch of a housing block. A left
turn down Blackshaw Road leads to
Wellgate, where a right turn up past the
Wheatsheaf Inn takes you to the centre of
Old Glossop. The route continues left
down Church Street past the church, then
left again along Shepley Street and past
old factory buildings to the start of the
bridleway known as Doctor's Gate.

The bridleway rises gently and after
1.5km you cross the bridge below Mossy
Lea Farm. For the next 3.5km the route
rises alongside Shelf Brook up onto the
Bleaklow plateau. You soon pass a stone
barn, where the bridleway bears to the
right, and after another 1km a footbridge
takes you across the brook, beyond which
the going becomes boggier and steeper.
After crossing Urchin Clough the route

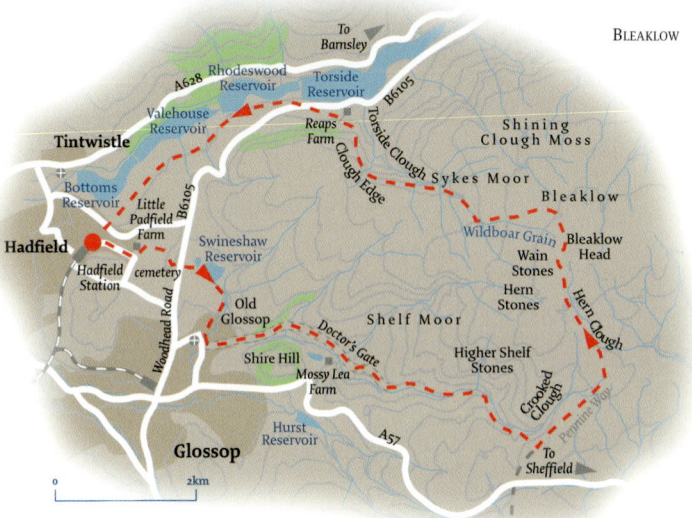

zigzags up the shoulder ahead to a gate and then levels off to reach the junction with the Pennine Way (PW). Here turn left along the PW for 1.2km where, just before the PW bears left uphill to a high point, there is a choice of routes.

The more adventurous can navigate with map and compass northwest over open moorland, leaving the route at a small slab with an arrow pointing left alongside a grough, crossing the headwaters of Crooked Clough towards the triangulation pillar at Higher Shelf Stones, before turning northeast past the 1948 crash site of a B-29 Superfortress, down through the peat hags to Hern Stones, up to Wain Stones and on to Bleaklow Head, with its large cairn and PW marker.

The more straightforward route, though still confusing in poor weather, keeps to the PW, heading northwards up to a high point, before tracking NNW for 2km down to Hern Clough and a twisting way up to the right of Wain Stones, finally turning right to the large cairn at Bleaklow Head.

At the large cairn ensure you turn left and descend gently NNW for 500m. The PW now heads westwards alongside Wildboar Grain, veering right after 1.1km opposite a side-stream and crossing to the left bank. Continue northwestwards and, 100m beyond a stile, fork right onto the lower path as the PW now heads westwards above Torside Clough, before rising and circling to the north along Clough Edge, and finally descending the grassy slope down to Reaps Farm. Here, bear left along the driveway to the Woodhead Road. Across the road lies the Longdendale Trail, where a left turn takes you back to Hadfield after 5km.

◀ Looking northeast from Doctor's Gate to Bleaklow Head

Kinder Scout

Distance 13.5km **Time** 5 hours
Terrain lanes, tracks and moorland paths,
with ascent of 600m **Map** OS Explorer OL1
Access buses from Glossop and Stockport
to Hayfield, 1.5km from the start

This is one of the best routes onto Kinder
Scout, and is celebrated for its place in
the history of the opening up of access to
large tracts of moorland.

The growth and industrialisation of
towns and cities in and around the Peak
District in the 19th century brought with
it great social change while the railways
brought greater movement of people.
On busy Sundays in the 1930s thousands
of people flocked from Manchester to
Hayfield Station and into conflict with
landowners and gamekeepers. Matters
came to a head on 24th April 1932 when
several hundred walkers met at Bowden
Bridge Quarry and headed up William
Clough. Known as the Mass Trespass, the
leaders of the protest were arrested and
jailed. Today, enshrined in law is the 'right

to roam' on Access Land and people can
walk the moorland unfettered.

The walk starts at Bowden Bridge
Quarry car park, 1km east of Hayfield, with
a memorial plaque on the crag at the rear.
Go up the lane beyond the car park, with
the River Kinder on the right, to Booth,
where there are sheep dip pens. Dogleg
over the bridge and after 75m fork left off
the lane onto a footpath, which takes you
through a gate into woods before
switching left back over the river in 200m.
Turn right and take the bridleway to the
left of Kinder Reservoir gates (SP White
Brow). The bridleway rises fairly steeply
by a wall and bends right. Where it turns
left, keep ahead on the path by the wall
and along the west side of the reservoir.

At the end of the reservoir, ignore the
footbridge to the right and keep ahead on
the left of the stream into William Clough.
The path criss-crosses its way over the
stream and can be muddy underfoot. After
1km, at a confluence, keep up the right-
hand stream as the going steepens to the

◄ Memorial plaque
in Bowden Bridge
Quarry car park

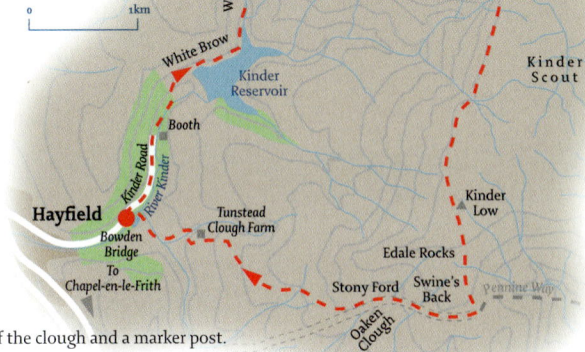

0   1km

Mill Hill

William Clough

Sandy Heys

Kinder
Downfall

Kinder
Scout

White Brow

Kinder
Reservoir

Booth

Kinder Road

River Kinder

Hayfield

Bowden
Bridge
To
Chapel-en-le-Frith

Tunstead
Clough Farm

Kinder
Low

Edale Rocks

Stony Ford

Swine's
Back

Pennine Way

Oaken Clough

top of the clough and a marker post.

The route now turns ESE along the
flagged Pennine Way and climbs the slope
ahead to a cairn, where the gradient eases.
It is now simple to follow the plateau-
edge path as it undulates southeastwards
for the next 2km over the bluff of Sandy
Heys and on to Kinder Downfall, with
good views down over the reservoir. Here,
the plateau-edge path turns SSW, in 1km
crossing the Red Brook and in another
600m rising to a cairn marking a fork in
the path. Here, the plateau-edge path veers
a little to the left (SSE) and in 400m passes
just west of the trig point of Kinder Low.

The route continues down in the same
direction for 500m past Edale Rocks to a
cairn marking the junction with the path
along the southern edge of the plateau.
Bear right past the rocky outcrop of the
Swine's Back and carry on down to the
wall and path junction. Here, leave the

Pennine Way, which descends to Edale,
and turn right along the stony bridleway
for 800m down to the stream at Stony
Ford above Oaken Clough.

Here, take the footpath off right (SP
Hayfield via Tunstead Clough) over a stile
into fields. Contour for 500m around the
shoulder of the hill to a fork in the path,
where you bear left downhill to a ladder
stile over the wall at a stream-head and the
limit of Access Land. The footpath now
descends over a series of fields, veering to
the right, and in the fourth field passes
along a wall to a gate. A left turn down two
more fields brings you to Tunstead Clough
Farm, from where a lane zigzags down
across a stream to a crossroads. Keep ahead
down the wooded lane which soon bends
left to reach the bridge by the campsite
opposite Bowden Bridge car park.

Derwent Edge and Back Tor

Distance 12.5km **Time** 4 hours
Terrain lanes, open moorland tracks and
paths with ascent of 400m
Map OS Explorer OL1 **Access** bus from
Sheffield and Castleton

**Wind your way down the side of
Ladybower Reservoir before climbing
onto Derwent Edge and its wind-
weathered tors.**

Mention the Derwent Reservoirs and
many people make the association with
617 Dambusters Squadron who trained
here for their attack on the Ruhr dams in
1943. Others recall that at the end of the
19th century the Derwent Valley Water
Board was established to build six
reservoirs to provide water for the cities of
Sheffield, Derby, Nottingham and
Leicester, though in the end only three

were built, Howden, Upper Derwent and
Ladybower, completed in the same year as
the Dambusters' raid. This last reservoir
also saw the villages of Derwent and
Ashopton drowned beneath the waters,
the villagers rehoused to the south at
Yorkshire Bridge, and the planting of large
tracts of conifers.

The walk starts from Fairholmes Visitor
Centre at the northern end of Ladybower
Reservoir. From the visitor centre's car
park take a path (SP The Dams) to the lane
between Ladybower and Upper Derwent
Reservoirs. Turn right onto this lane
which heads past the towers of Derwent
Dam and turns southeastwards for 1.5km
before bending to the left and the inlet of
Mill Brook, where it becomes a gravel
path. Continue for another 300m and just
before a road-gate take the bridleway off
left (SP Derwent Edge to Moscar) up the
field and beside Grindle Clough to the
shelter of Grindle Barn.

From here the bridleway crosses the
clough and in 150m veers left up beside a
pine plantation to a gate onto open

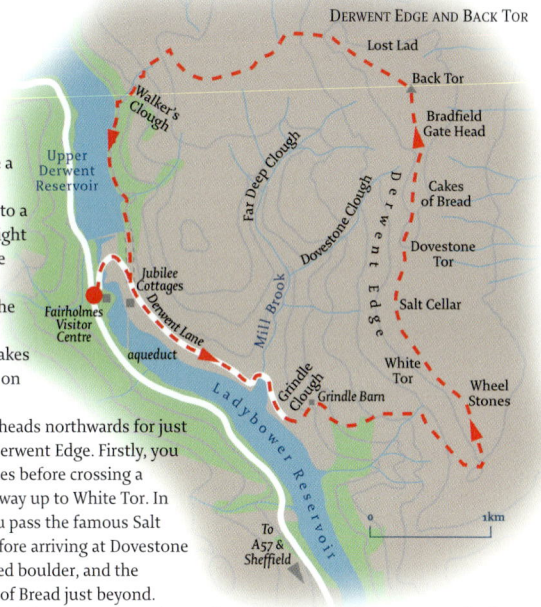

moorland, before a rising traverse of 500m brings you to a wall. Here, turn right for 50m alongside the wall before heading left off the bridleway onto a footpath which takes you up to a cairn on Derwent Edge.

The route now heads northwards for just over 3km along Derwent Edge. Firstly, you reach Wheel Stones before crossing a slight dip on the way up to White Tor. In another 500m you pass the famous Salt Cellar boulder before arriving at Dovestone Tor, with its arched boulder, and the weathered Cakes of Bread just beyond. Flagstones now lead the way over a path junction at Bradfield Gate Head up to the triangulation pillar on top of Back Tor.

From Back Tor, make sure you take the left fork northwestwards across the small dip to the cairn and topograph of grassy Lost Lad. The route continues northwestwards for another 250m before veering left and descending in a westwards direction for 400m to a level area and a path junction. Here, fork left onto a thinner path, which soon curves a little to the right and becomes more distinct as it joins the footpath from Bradfield Gate Head to bring you in another 150m to a stone wall. After a further 100m, fork right to stay on the

footpath which leads to a gate and stile. The footpath now bears right and drops gently northwestwards by a wall to a fingerpost after 250m: this points the way left downhill just before the next wall. Head over the next cross-paths, beyond which the path descends more steeply as it zigzags its way down into Walker's Clough. Here, in the corner of two walls, a gate into the woodland beyond leads you down to Upper Derwent Reservoir.

A left turn along the reservoir-edge path brings you back to the dam after 1km, where a footpath off right through a small gate just before the end of the reservoir takes you back down to the lane which leads to the visitor centre.

◀ Wheel Stones on Derwent Edge

Crook Hill

Distance 6km **Time** 2 hours
Terrain tracks, fields and grassy hillside
Map OS Explorer OL1 **Access** bus from
Sheffield and Castleton (Fearfall Wood or
Bridge End stops)

**A walk with the perfect mix of water,
woodland and hilltop views.**

The walk starts from Hurst Clough car
park beside the northern section of
Ladybower Reservoir, 1.2km north of the
A57 Snake Road. Head out of the back of
the car park and down the bank, turn left
onto the footpath, over Hurst Clough on a
footbridge, and then keep alongside the
reservoir through woods for 1km. Just
before a gate and fence, head back up
across the road to Bridge End car park
(which makes for an alternative start at
busy periods).

Head up the bridleway, which rises
steeply at first, easing off after 500m, up
to a gate and path junction with the old
packhorse route to Glossop. The route
turns left here (SP Crookhill Farm) onto
the field-edge bridleway alongside the
forestry plantation over Bridge-end
Pasture. The improved grassland of the
pasture is a stark contrast to the
surrounding moorland of the Derwent
Valley. After 500m, at the end of the
forestry, continue southeastwards uphill
through a gate in a wall to the top of the
rise. From here, you can see the twin tors
of Crook Hill ahead while to the right
there is a view all the way up Edale. Just
south of the high point, though off the
right-of-way, are the well-preserved
remains of a Bronze Age round cairn – it is
thought to be a funerary mound and not
known to have been excavated.

Now descend for 400m to reach a fork in
the bridleway. The left fork heads for
Crookhill Farm and can be followed if you

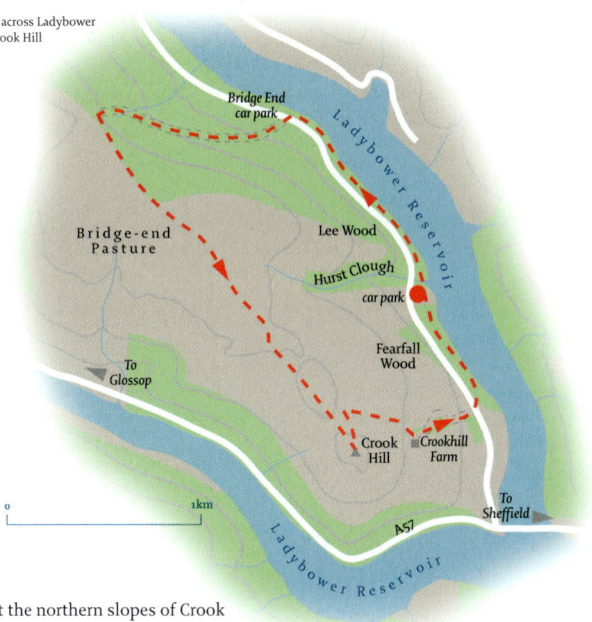

◄ Looking north across Ladybower Reservoir to Crook Hill

wish to skirt the northern slopes of Crook Hill, but to reach the tops take the right fork (SP Snake Road) for 100m to the next gate, which marks the entrance to Access Land. From here, veer left down to the base of the hill and pick your way up. A little clambering on the rocky outcrops is possible for a more sporting way to the tops, of which the first is the higher.

From the dip between the tops, head east to pick up the bridleway 150m north of Crookhill Farm. Here, an alternative signed route for walkers avoids the working farmyard by skirting below it. Go through the wall-gate and descend diagonally down the field. At the far side, turn left (off the alternative route for walkers) and follow the bridleway once more for 300m down to the road where a left turn takes you back to the start after 600m. If you don't fancy the hard surface, after 100m just past the road gates you can zigzag down a grassy woodland track to use the kinder reservoir-edge path.

19

Lantern Pike

Distance 5.5km **Time** 2 hours
Terrain old railway track, fields and open
moorland with some steep ascent
Map OS Explorer OL1 **Access** bus from
Glossop, Buxton and Huddersfield

**Follow the beautiful Sett Valley before
climbing to the summit of shapely
Lantern Pike.**

The walk starts in the village of Hayfield
at the Countryside Centre car park, which
has an information centre. You can also
spend time walking around Hayfield itself
and there is a short signed walk, the
Calico Trail, which traces the town's
industrial past.

This route heads out of the rear of
the car park for 1.3km along the Sett
Valley Trail, a disused railway line to
Manchester, which also carries the
Pennine Bridleway. This flat and lightly
wooded section is pleasant and leads

you past Bluebell Wood Nature Reserve
to Birch Vale Reservoir.

At the far end of the reservoir, turn right
(SP Lantern Pike) onto a footpath across
the dam and the River Sett up into fields.
A marker-post shows the way uphill to a
gate into a fenced walkway up to a lane.
Here, turn left uphill for 150m to a
junction with the Pennine Bridleway
(PBW) and then right for 300m up to a
lane. Dogleg right, then left across the
lane to continue more steeply up the
PBW, past the entrance to Upper Cliffe
Farm, above which the track becomes
stony and twists its way up to a gate into
the High Peak Estate land of Lantern Pike,
owned by the National Trust and
designated as Access Land, with good
views right up to Kinder.

At this point the PBW continues over
the eastern side of the hill, but to reach
the top of Lantern Pike turn left beyond

◀ Across the Sett Valley from the slopes of Lantern Pike

the gate for a short but steep pull up alongside a wall, before bearing right up the hill's southern ridge to the top, marked by a memorial topograph to the access campaigner Edwin Royce. To continue, descend the north ridge and, at the limit of Access Land, pick up the PBW again to a gate. Just beyond, where the PBW veers left, cut down to the right to a stile to pick up a footpath, which heads down the field beyond beside a wall and Hey Wood to reach a cottage and a track.

Here, turn right along the track past the cottage, ignoring the footpath to Little Hayfield, to reach Cliffbank Farm and continue down for another 200m to a bend. Keep ahead onto the bridleway along the edge of woodland for 200m,

before forking left off the bridleway onto a footpath which takes you down to some cottages and onto Bank Vale Road. Continue over a rise to the junction with Swallow House Lane. Turn left here and continue for 200m until just before the A624 flyover bridge, where you should turn right onto a footpath across Old School Field. At the far end bear right across the footbridge over the River Sett, then left along the riverside walkway to some steps up into a housing estate. Here, a left turn takes you back to Hayfield Countryside Centre.

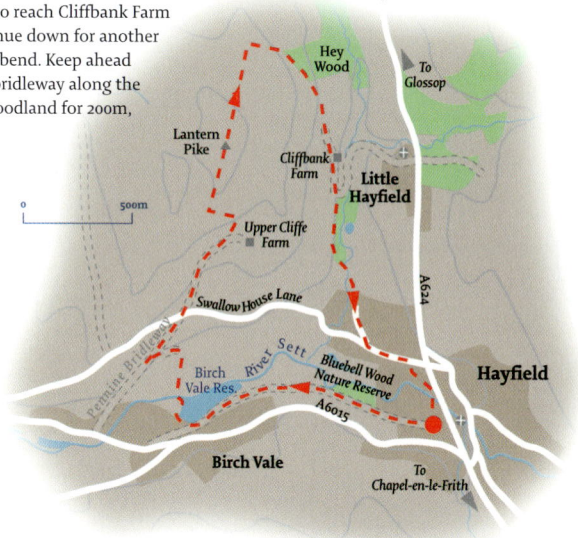

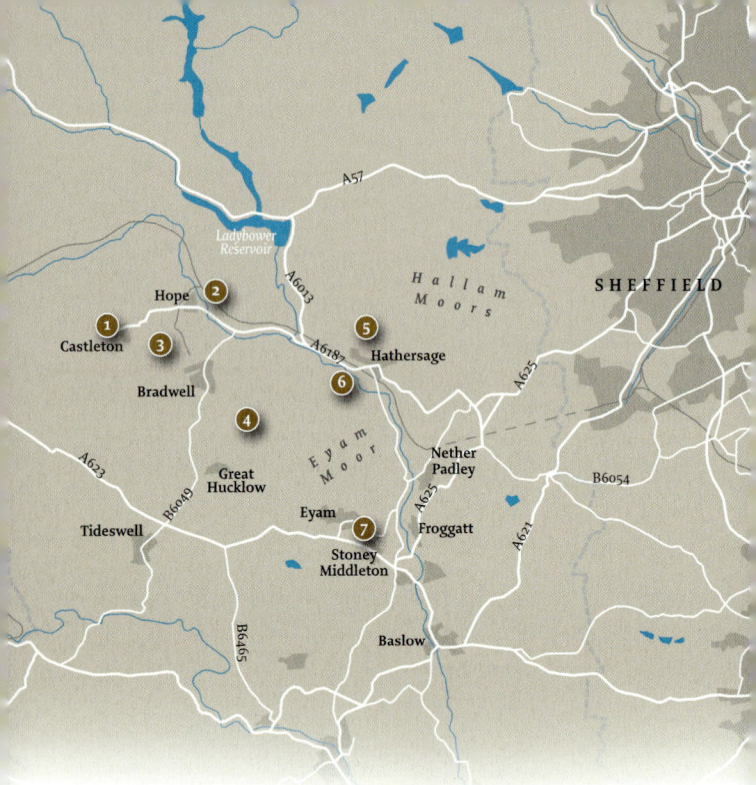

A57

Ladybower
Reservoir

*H a l l a m
M o o r s*

SHEFFIELD

Hope ②

②

①
Castleton

③

A6013

A6187

⑤
Hathersage

Bradwell

⑥

④

*E y a m
M o o r*

A625

A623

**Great
Hucklow**

B6049

**Nether
Padley**

B6054

Tideswell

Eyam

A625

Froggatt

⑦
**Stoney
Middleton**

A621

B6465

Baslow

Castleton lies at the western end of
the Hope Valley and is one of the most
popular places in the Peak. Noted for its
medieval castle and show caves, it sits
on the boundary of the Dark and White
Peak. To the north lies the 'shivering
mountain' of Mam Tor with its great
ridge running west to east to Lose Hill
and Win Hill beyond.

To the south, beyond Cave Dale, rises
the grass-covered limestone plateau while
further east gritstone still predominates.
The River Derwent flows past the pretty
village of Hathersage and its famous
Stanage Edge on its journey towards
Baslow. This borderland, where gritstone
vies with limestone, rough grazing moor
with grass-rich pasture, gives some of the
best walking when the high routes over
the moors are covered in cloud, and there
is plenty to see and visit if wet boots have
lost their appeal.

Above Winnats Head looking southeastwards ▶

Castleton and the Heart of the Peak District

The Great Ridge

Distance 14km **Time** 4 hours 30
Terrain lanes, tracks and an exposed ridge
with 600m of ascent **Map** OS Explorer OL1
Access train to Edale from Manchester
and Sheffield

**A classic and popular route which takes
in one of the best ridgelines in the Peak.**

Edale lies in a broad valley between
Kinder Scout and the Dark Peak to the
north and Mam Tor and the White Peak to
the south. It has long drawn walkers and
ramblers and it also marks the southern
end of the Pennine Way, the long-distance
trail which heads north for more than
400km to the Scottish Borders. This walk,
however, heads south to what has
become known as the Great Ridge.

There is a car park at the southern edge
of Edale village, more properly known as
Grindsbrook Booth, a short distance from
the railway station. From the car park

head towards the centre of the village
and turn left up the access road to the
railway station. A concessionary path
(SP Barber Booth) takes you on through
the railway yard onto a grassy track. In
100m bear left into a field and then turn
right to continue parallel to the railway.
At the end of the field keep ahead up a
track which soon bends right, across
the railway. Once over the bridge bear
left along a grassy track for 75m before
taking the gate on the right and then
circling back to the left to join a public
footpath heading southwestwards over
four fields. The route now turns left,
back over the railway, into the hamlet of
Barber Booth.

At the lane turn right past cottages to
the road, continue across the bridge over
the River Noe and take the first lane off to
the right towards Upper Booth. After
200m the route heads off to the left onto a

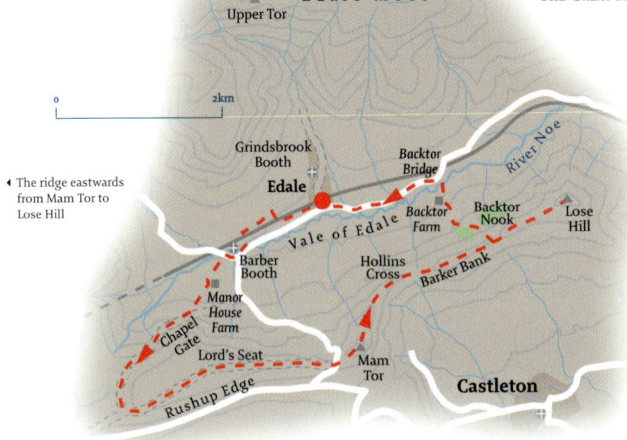

Edale Moor

Upper Tor

Grindsbrook Booth

Backtor Bridge

River Noe

Edale

Vale of Edale

Backtor Farm

Backtor Nook

Lose Hill

◄ The ridge eastwards from Mam Tor to Lose Hill

Barber Booth

Hollins Cross

Barker Bank

Manor House Farm

Chapel Gate

Lord's Seat

Rushup Edge

Mam Tor

Castleton

footpath up a field alongside a stream and across a farm track, before circling to the right of Manor House Farm. Beyond, the path follows the fenceline up rougher pasture to Chapel Gate.

This well-defined byway rises steeply at first before the gradient eases and then heads southwards, descending gently past the path from Brown Knoll and on for another 500m to a junction with a bridleway at a drystone wall. A left turn onto the bridleway takes you gently uphill for 1.2km: the bridleway switches to the right of the wall, but keep on the left where a footpath leads up to the broad top of Lord's Seat and its Bronze Age barrow. From here Rushup Edge becomes more defined as it sweeps down to the gap below Mam Tor and gives some of the best walking in the Peak.

The route continues across the road and heads up steps on the well-trodden path to the triangulation point on top of Mam Tor. Descend the north ridge, where the path is initially flagged, and in just over 1km you reach the dip of Hollins Cross. Continue along the ridge for another 800m, over the rise of Barker Bank and down to the path junction at Backtor Nook. This point marks the descent off the ridge back to Edale, but to reach Lose Hill you continue out and back along the ridge for a further 1km, heading steeply up Back Tor before a more undulating section leads you to the final rise to Lose Hill, marked by a topograph.

To descend from Backtor Nook, take the path northwestwards which in 250m crosses a stone wall (SP Backtor Bridge) and in a further 250m picks up another wall down to a gate, where the bridleway from Hollins Cross joins. Continue down past Backtor Farm, along the lane over Backtor Bridge and bear left up to the valley road. Turn left along the road to pass Mill Cottages, arriving back at Edale after 1.4km.

Win Hill

Distance 7.5km **Time** 2 hours 30
Terrain lanes and open moorland, with
a cumulative ascent of 300m
Map OS Explorer OL1 **Access** Hope Station
is 1km east of the village centre; buses to
Hope from Castleton, Sheffield, Bakewell
and Chesterfield

**Stride out on this easy hill walk – it
makes a great outing for children and is
one of the best viewpoints in the Peak.**

Hope is one of the oldest villages in the
Peak District and, while it may not draw
the crowds that head up the Hope Valley
to Castleton, it is well worth a visit. There
is also plenty of history, or myth, to the
place. The first king of all England,
Athelstan, fought a battle here in 926 and
before him, in the 1st century AD, the
Romans had built a fort to the southeast.
St Peter's Church was rebuilt during the
14th century and there are three crosses, a
preaching cross, the shaft of a Saxon cross
and a medieval market cross. There is also
the tradition of how Win Hill and Lose
Hill, its neighbour across the Noe Valley,
gained their names. Some interpretations
favour an etymological explanation, Win
in origin meaning 'willow', Lose
indicating an 'enclosure'. Others trace this
to a battle between the kings of Mercia
and Northumbria in the 7th century. More
certain are the offerings in the village's
cafés and pubs.

From the centre of the village of Hope,
opposite St Peter's Church, head up Edale
Road for 350m. At the bend, fork right
(SP Cemetery & Twitchill Farm) down
Bowden Lane to the bridge over the River
Noe. Ignoring footpaths off to the right,

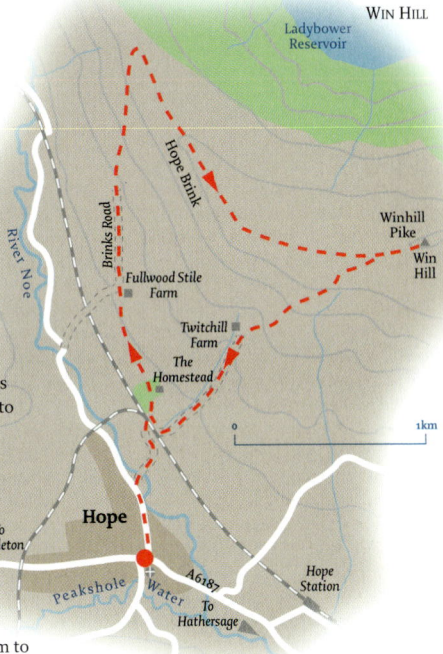

continue up the tree-lined lane, which soon passes under the railway and bears left. At the end of the lane, fork left in front of house-gates onto a footpath which leads you up the driveway to a house and into the fields beyond. The route now heads over two fields to the buildings of Fullwood Stile Farm and onto the lane of Brinks Road beyond, which rises gently for 500m to the gate to Access Land.

Beyond the gate immediately fork right off the bridleway onto a footpath which makes a rising traverse up the bracken moorland for 700m to the top of the broad ridge, just short of a forestry plantation, with increasingly good views southwards over the Hope Valley and westwards to Lose Hill, Mam Tor, Edale and Kinder Plateau. A right turn now takes you onto a permissive path which heads southeastwards along the ridge for the next 1km before bearing left alongside a wall and past the plateau's western top to the final rise to the craggy tor of Win Hill. On a clear day, the reward for your efforts is a great view northwards over Ladybower Reservoir to Derwent's edges and watershed.

To continue, retrace your steps for 250m to the first kissing-gate and turn left onto a footpath for a descending traverse southwestwards over the moorland, with views across the Hope Valley to Bradwell and Castleton, with Pin Dale and Cave Dale prominent. After 200m you pass a cairn and go over a stone wall where the gradient steepens for the next 350m to a stile at the edge of Access Land. A descent down two fields soon brings you to Twitchill Farm, beyond which the route follows its driveway for 700m to a junction with Bowden Lane. Here, turn left under the railway bridge to retrace the outward route back to Hope.

◀ From the western slopes of Win Hill across the Noe Valley to Lose Hill

27

Castleton

Distance 7km **Time** 2 hours 15
Terrain paths, tracks, narrow roads
Map OS Explorer OL1 **Access** bus to
Castleton from Sheffield, Chesterfield
and Bakewell

**When you have had your fill of the
attractions of one of the Peak District's
most popular towns, try this easy walk
– perfect for an evening stroll or for an
outing with children.**

It is rare not to find Castleton busy with
tourists, drawn to the town for its
dramatic location at the head of the Hope
Valley below the shifting shales of Mam
Tor and Peveril Castle set on its near-
impregnable perch of limestone since the
Norman period. However, this town also
has a long industrial history. Treak Cliff,
Speedwell, Peak Cavern and Blue John
mines are now show caves open to the
public but are also a reminder of the
mining for lead ores dating from the time
of the Roman occupation and, since the
mid-18th century, for fluorospar, known
locally as Blue John – calcium fluoride, the
chief source of fluorine for the chemical
industry, which is used in the
manufacture of Teflon, anaesthetics,
toothpaste and aluminium.

From the centre of Castleton by Ye Olde
Nags Head walk up Back Street (SP Peveril
Castle & Cave Dale). At the triangular
Market Place keep left up Pindale Road for
50m, before turning right for Cave Dale
along the Limestone Way (LW).

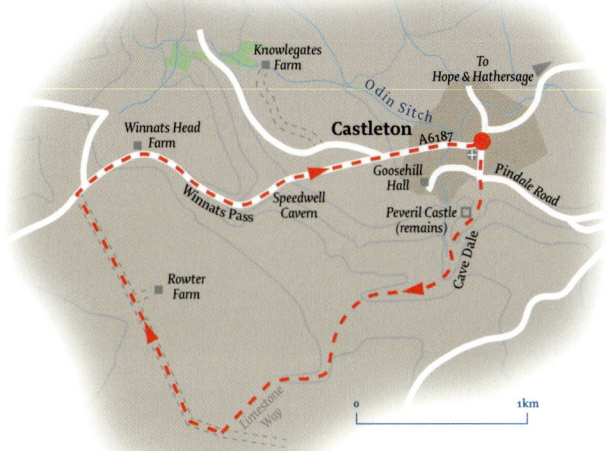

0   1km

Here, the path squeezes its way between limestone crags and for the next 1.5km winds its way up the grassy dale, which soon opens out as you gain height, with Peveril Castle high up on the right and views back to Win Hill. It brings you to a gate in a wall where the LW bears right and in 200m passes through another wall, before veering left at a path junction. From here continue for 500m, over the crest of a small rise and past a little pond to a large gate with stone wall-steps in the corner of the field at a cross-paths with the byway from Pin Dale.

At the cross-paths, turn right up the byway and in 200m bear right at the bend, in a NNW direction, with the land-slipped face of Mam Tor visible ahead. The track, which can be muddy, rises gently and passes between old quarries and mine-workings on the left and the entrance to

Rowter Farm, before dropping down for 700m to the road.

Turn right along the road and then in 75m keep right at the bend (SP Castleton, Caves, Peveril Castle). The road soon starts to descend past Winnats Head Farm, beyond which you can step off the tarmac and follow the pleasant grassy verge on the left down through the limestone cliffs of Winnats Pass itself. You may well see climbers scrambling up the steep craggy ridges of this collapsed former cave, or lower down you might be tempted underground to explore the subterranean passages of Speedwell Cavern.

From here you can either take the roadside walkway for 1km back into Castleton or the more scenic footpath which heads off right and contours its way round the hillside above Goosehill Hall to the upper part of the town.

Shatton Moor

Distance 8.5km **Time** 2 hours 30
Terrain lanes and byways, with some
steep ascent and descent
Map OS Explorer OL1
Access Bamford Station lies 500m east of
the start; buses to Shatton from
Sheffield, Bakewell and Chesterfield

A quieter route up onto the moorland
above the village of Shatton, which lies
midway between Hathersage and Hope,
just off the A6187 across the River Noe.

Head up through the pretty village of
Shatton, past two lanes on the left, to a
ford just beyond Wheat Hay Farm.
Continue along the delightful Townfield
Lane, rising gently and passing Townfield
Barn, with intermittent views right to Win
Hill and left to Shatton Moor. There is an
alternative footpath up on the bank
alongside this ancient holloway, which
follows the old saltway route to Brough
and beyond. It is usually peaceful, but if
you visit in mid-March you might well
find yourself caught up in the rush of
Shatton Fell Race.

After 800m at a gate the lane becomes a
byway. Continue for another 300m and, at
the top of the rise, turn left off the byway
onto the footpath that follows the track
to Elmore Hill Farm. At the farm, go past
the cowsheds and keep an eye on the
footpath which heads through a gate on
the right. Beyond, climb the left side of
the field alongside the wall and over the
brow to Brough Lane, with the reward of a
long view down the Hope Valley.

Turn left onto the byway of Brough
Lane, which climbs steeply at times as it
winds its way for the next 1.5km up to its
high point, before sweeping left round
the head of Over Dale to meet the top of
the lane up from Abney. Continue
northeastwards along the now grassier

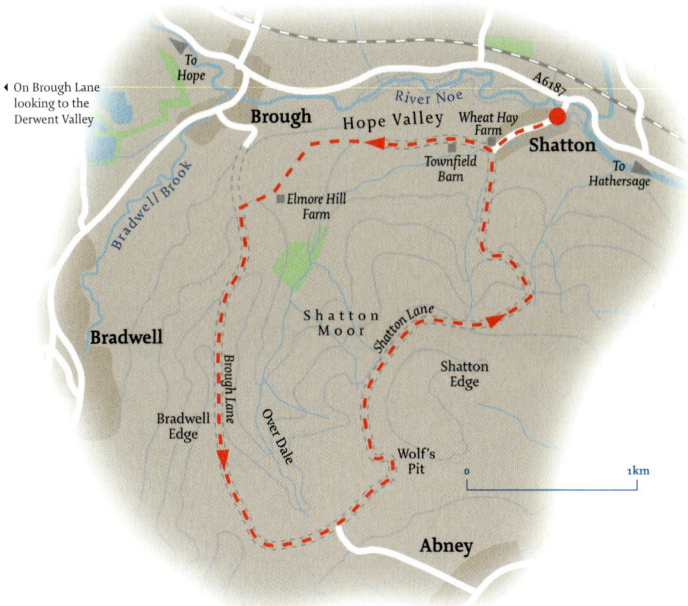

◄ On Brough Lane
looking to the
Derwent Valley

byway (SP Shatton) for 400m to the edge of Access Land, beyond which rises Abney Moor to the east. At this point ensure you stay on the byway as it circles back round to the west, past Wolf's Pit, before turning sharp right (SP Shatton) onto the byway of Shatton Lane. Of course, wolves have long gone from the Peak District, but some survived into Tudor times and their memory is hinted at in place names such as Woolow and Wooler. Shatton Lane is a reminder of more recent changes as it was probably created in the mid-19th century during the enclosure of much of the surrounding land. The only thing to watch out for now are packs of rogue off-roaders, and, in season, the flora that lines the lane.

Now heading northwards, the byway contours round the Access Land limit of Shatton Moor before rising gently to the communications mast, with views to Win Hill, Mam Tor, Kinder and the Bleaklow plateau. From here the homeward descent begins in earnest. After 700m the byway turns sharp left and becomes a lane which continues downhill for 1km to take you back down to Wheat Hay Farm in Shatton. Here, a right turn leads you back through the centre of the village.

31

High Neb and Stanage Edge

Distance 12km **Time** 3 hours 30 **Terrain** fields, open moorland and cliff edges, 400m of steady ascent in the first half **Map** OS Explorer OL1 **Access** train from Manchester and Nottingham, bus from Castleton, Sheffield and Chesterfield

A longer approach to one of the Peak District's most famous edges from one of its best-known villages.

From the centre of Hathersage just above The Square walk along Baulk Lane (SP Church) past houses and the church. The lane soon narrows and starts to rise before entering fields. The footpath continues to rise gently to a high point, beyond which keep left at the fork with the track to Cow Close, descend past the buildings of Brookfield Manor and cross a stream on the way up to Birley Lane.

The route continues northwards across the next field before entering woodland. In 150m fork left across the bridge over Hood Brook (SP Dennis Knoll via Green's House). The path now climbs to the top of the wood and then up three more fields to Green's House. Here, dogleg left for 30m, then right up beside a stream into open moorland. After 100m, keep right with the footpath which continues gently up to the right of a wall to the road below Stanage Edge, by Dennis Knoll plantation. A left turn on the road takes you to a car park and junction with a byway. Just east of here archaeologists have identified the remains of a Bronze Age settlement, with cairns, the markings of stone-walled huts and field systems. It must have been bleak living, even with some protection afforded by Stanage Edge.

Turn right for 500m along the byway and beside a small plantation – 5m beyond its far edge look out for a ladder stile on the left to take you up through grass and bracken to a junction with the main path, marked by a millstone and boulder,

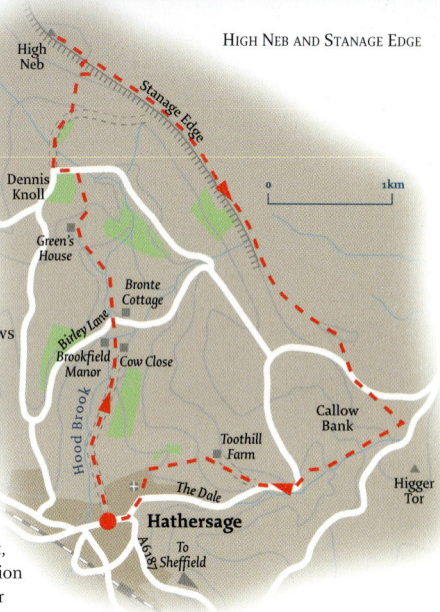

◂ Outcrops on Stanage Edge

running along the base of the rocks of Stanage Edge. Here, dogleg right for 50m, then left to pick up a path which curves right up to the top. A detour left for 350m takes you to the trig point of High Neb and good views towards Win Hill and Edale.

The onward route turns right to head southeastwards along Stanage Edge for the next 3km – dogleg left, then right to keep to the top-edge path where the byway comes up from the right after 1km for the best views and to see climbers topping out, before the rise to the triangulation point at the far end. Quarries for millstones and grindstones dot the landscape here, a reminder of the industry that the gritstone edges provided since at least the 15th century.

To descend, retrace your steps from the trig point for 50m to follow a path southeastwards towards and then alongside the road to a slight high point. Cross the road and the stile opposite to follow the left hand of three grassy paths for 300m before picking up a footpath which, just before another road, heads southwestwards down between Higger Tor and the knoll of Callow Bank. This area was used for leadmining in the 18th century with coal-fired cupolas – furnaces with high chimneys instead of powered bellows to provide sufficient draught for the smelting process. At the edge of Access Land, the route takes the same line for 500m along the byway, passing over a stream and up to the road. Continue left down the road for 300m and then take the footpath to the right.

Just before Toothill Farm branch left into fields – cross the first, head diagonally down the second, then straight down the third to a stile into the tree-lined holloway. Further down this becomes a lane which meanders past cottages to a junction with Church Bank lane. At this point, you can detour to the parish church and Little John's grave or continue left down to the road junction with The Dale, where a right turn takes you back to the main road at the top end of Hathersage.

33

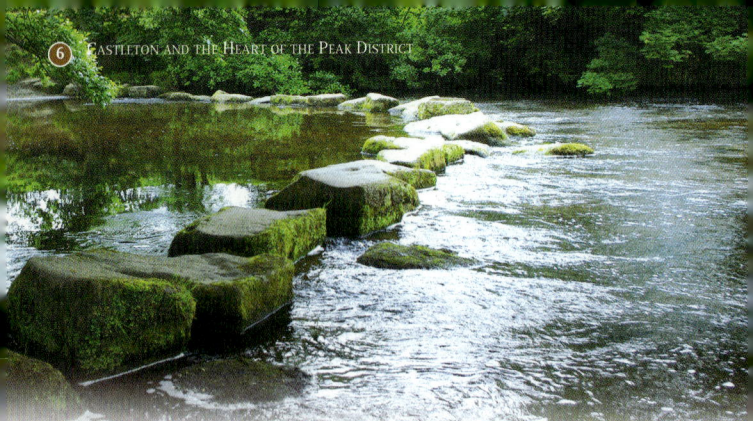

Hathersage and Offerton Moor

Distance 7.5km **Time** 2 hours
Terrain lanes, footpaths and byways
Map OS Explorer OL1 **Access** train from
Manchester and Nottingham, bus from
Castleton, Sheffield and Chesterfield

**A lesser-known stroll, ideal for when
the clouds are down or there is need of
some gentler scenery.**

The village of Hathersage is one of the
most popular Peak District villages.
Aficionados of local lore will want to see
Little John's grave in the churchyard,
though the nearby medieval ringwork of
Camp Green is on firmer historical ground
than the Robin Hood myth, even if his
cave on Stanage Edge and birthplace of
Loxley are not too far away.

Lovers of Charlotte Brontë are drawn to
the village's novelistic association with
the Eyres, but in the middle of the 19th
century the working mills in the village's
wire, needle and button industry made
for a grimmer, and grimier, reality than

one might expect from how the streets
look today. The mills closed and the
railway arrived just over a hundred years
ago and led to the establishment of a
still-thriving tourist trade.

From the centre of Hathersage at the
junction of the A6187 with the B6001
head down the lane to the right of
The Little John Hotel, alongside Hood
Brook, and under the railway viaduct to
the lodge and entrance to Nether Hall.
At the bend here, turn right off the lane
(SP Leadmill Bridge) onto a footpath
which crosses two large fields along their
right-hand edge to reach the B6001 just
short of the late 18th-century Leadmill
Bridge, on the old turnpike road to
Grindleford. (If starting from the train
station, there is a pavement alongside the
B6001 to the bridge.)

On the far side of the bridge, turn right
into the meadows alongside the River
Derwent. After 200m you pass a weir and
soon after enter Goose Nest Wood. The

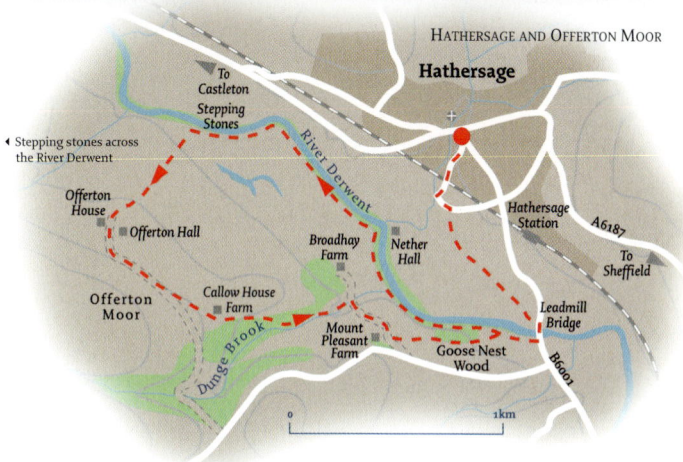

◀ Stepping stones across the River Derwent

path here is delightful, though close to the water and prone to flooding when the river is high. At the far side of the wood cross over Dunge Brook and two footbridges with fields on your left to reach a sharp left bend in the river opposite Nether Hall. Keep alongside the next straight slow-flowing section of river to a second bend and then in another 400m you reach a cross-paths, marked by a fingerpost, with Offerton signed off to the left and stepping stones to the right across the river, which makes a good spot for a rest or picnic.

From here, turn left across the meadow and up two fields to reach a fenced section up to Offerton and the footpath junction with a byway. A left turn onto the twisting byway takes you up past Offerton House and Offerton Hall. The byway now bends left again to pass above the Hall and heads alongside the lower edge of Offerton Moor, rising gently for 250m to a field gate. Just past this, take the footpath off left for

a descending traverse down a steep-sided field, over a stream and down to the buildings at Callow.

Now turn left down past Callow House Farm and into a field on a footpath which leads down to a gate into Callow Wood below. Here, a clear path drops down through the trees to Dunge Brook. At the far side of the wood go through the gate into a field, where the footpath continues down to a junction with a track. A right turn over Dunge Brook and up the track for 250m brings you to the top of the rise. Here, opposite the entrance to Mount Pleasant Farm, take the footpath off to the left into fields, heading down the middle of the first one and alongside the top edge of Goose Nest Wood.

Near the end of the second field, cross the wall on stone steps and descend the bank to reach the meadow beside the River Derwent, where you can bear right to rejoin the outward route back to Leadmill Bridge and Hathersage.

35

Eyam and Stoney Middleton

Distance 4km **Time** 1 hour 15
Terrain lanes and byways
Map OS Explorer OL24
Access buses to Eyam from Buxton,
Sheffield and Chesterfield

**A short but energetic route between
 exquisite villages.**

The village of Eyam needs little
introduction. Its place in the history of
the Great Plague of 1665-6 is well known,
not least because of the attempts of the
local rector, William Mompesson, to
confine the spread of the disease. The
fuller story is told in Eyam Museum,
opposite the car park, along with other
aspects of the village's history, the
establishment of its cotton, silk and shoe-
making industry, the effects of the area's
lead-mining and details of daily life over
the centuries.

From the south side of The Square in
the centre of Eyam head up The Lydgate, a
narrow lane which leads between cottages
and past the Lydgate Graves on the right.
At the top of the rise fork left down Mill
Lane and descend past cottages. Lower
down the lane becomes rougher
underfoot as its old walls twist their way
down through woodland to a gate at the
bottom. The route continues down out of
the woodland to a low point, with open
fields on the right and views ahead to
Froggatt and Curbar Edges, before
climbing over a small rise to descend
on a tarmac lane into Stoney Middleton.

At the junction turn left to head down
to the lower end of the village and the

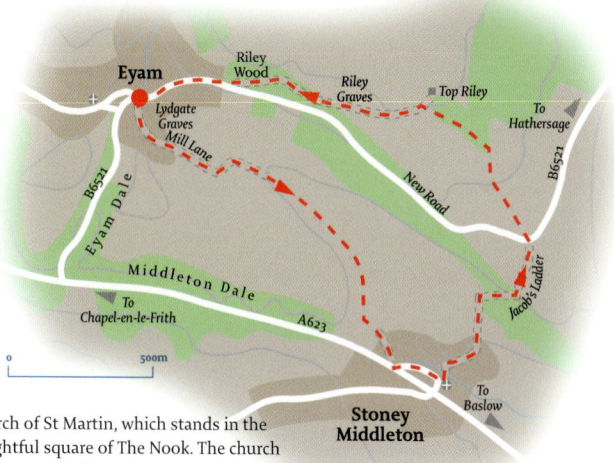

Church of St Martin, which stands in the delightful square of The Nook. The church presents something of a surprise. Its rare octagonal nave in Palladian 'rotunda' style was built after a fire in the 18th century and joined to the square medieval tower.

The route continues past the church and along the meandering lane. Here, on the left, you will find a 'Roman Bathhouse' with the Bath Gardens behind and a warm roadside spring just beyond. Although the Romans occupied the area and mined lead on the moors above the village, the actual building was constructed in the early 19th century on the orders of the Denman family, whose family home was the Jacobean Hall behind the church. Nevertheless, it is easy to see why people over two millennia have been drawn to the healing spring, and St Martin, conveniently, is the patron saint of cripples.

At the bend ahead bear left and ready yourself for a steep climb, known perhaps appropriately by some as Jacob's Ladder, as the lane zigzags its way up past the graveyard and through woodland to New Road, from where you can gain a direct view across to Froggatt and Curbar Edges.

Here, the climbing is not yet finished as you head across the road and take the path up between fields to a gate at the edge of the woodland. The route now bears left up past a rocky outcrop to reach a path junction. A left turn takes you up along the southern edge of the wood to a lane.

With the climb over the view opens out as you turn left down the lane, in 200m passing the Riley Graves in the field on the right. From here, it is a leisurely stroll of just less than 1km down the lane through Riley Wood to the road back into Eyam.

◀ The Riley Graves above Eyam

37

The numbered markers on the map are labeled 1 through 9.

Macclesfield Canal

Whaley Bridge

Chapel-en-le-Frith

A6

A623

B5470

Bollington

Fernilee Reservoir

Errwood Reservoir

A6

Tideswell

Macclesfield

A537

Buxton

Ridgegate Reservoir

A54

A53

A515

A5270

B5053

Longnor

A523

Tittesworth Reservoir

Leek

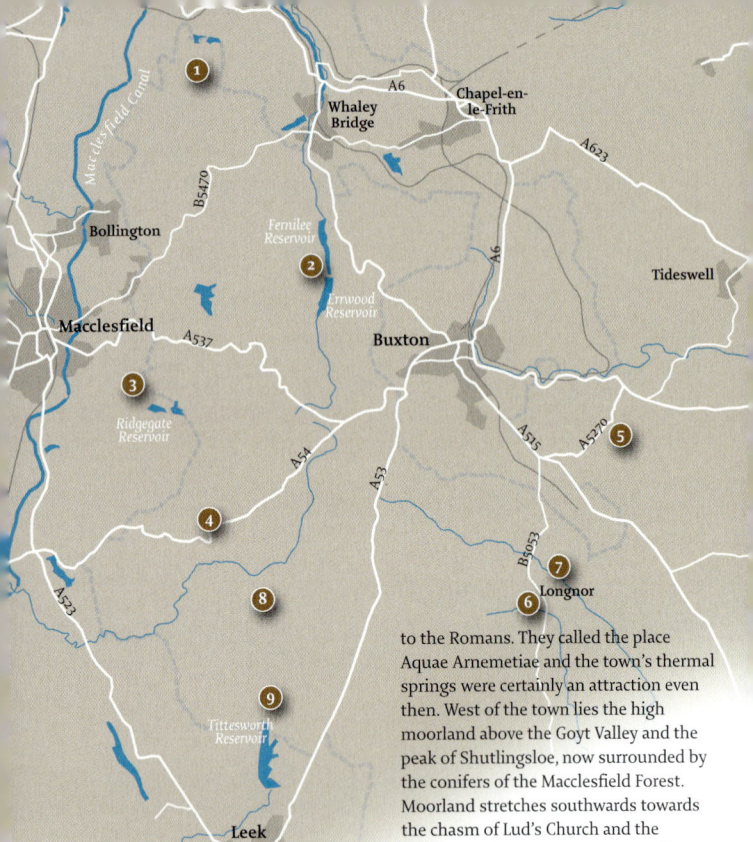

The former spa town of Buxton is the main town of the Peak, though it lies outside the national park, ringed as it is by limestone quarries. Its 18th- and 19th-century architecture is impressive and, standing at more than 300m above sea level, lays claim to be the highest town in England. Its history stretches back at least

to the Romans. They called the place Aquae Arnemetiae and the town's thermal springs were certainly an attraction even then. West of the town lies the high moorland above the Goyt Valley and the peak of Shutlingsloe, now surrounded by the conifers of the Macclesfield Forest. Moorland stretches southwards towards the chasm of Lud's Church and the millstone grit outcrops of The Roaches above the town of Leek. In contrast, to the east lies limestone. The River Wye races its way east in its dramatic gorge, while to its south are found the surprisingly steep-sided hills of the Upper Dove and the rectilinear drystone walls of the fields and villages of Chelmorton and Taddington high on the limestone plateau.

Hen Cloud from near Meerbrook ▶

Buxton and the West

Lyme Park and Sponds Hill

Distance 9km **Time** 2 hours 30
Terrain parkland and moorland with two
ascents **Map** OS Explorer OL1 **Access** free
bus service from the Park & Ride at Hazel
Grove, 7km from Lyme Park (Sundays and
Bank Holidays only)

**Climb over the park and moorland
surrounding one of Britain's most
famous houses.**

The walk starts from the National Trust
car park at Lyme Hall, which is accessed
from the A6 near Disley. Originally a
hunting lodge and home to the Legh
family for 600 years, the house and park
have been owned by the National Trust
since 1946. The house is one of the area's
main attractions and few can fail to be
impressed by the grand Palladian style,
especially the striking Ionic portico on the
south front. Inside, the Lyme Missal,
printed by William Caxton in 1487, is on
display at the centre of its own exhibition,
while the formal gardens, historic

parkland and surrounding moorland are
equally worth exploring.

Head up the steps to the left of the car
park, past both the main entrance and the
neoclassical façade of the Stables beyond,
where a track on the right takes you down
the side of this building into parkland and
along the high perimeter fence of the
Fallow Deer Park to a wall at the start of
open moorland and Access Land.

Once over the ladder stile, a steady
ascent takes you up alongside Lantern
Wood and past an old quarry to another
wall at the top of the rise. Here, turn right
for 400m up to the top, which carries a
topograph and a memorial to the
Monkhouse family.

The onward route is now visible ahead
on the skyline. Continue down beside the
wall for 300m to a track junction near the
cottage at Bowstonegate and turn left
past the cottage to the lane. The Bow
Stones themselves, upper parts of Saxon
crosses thought to have been placed here

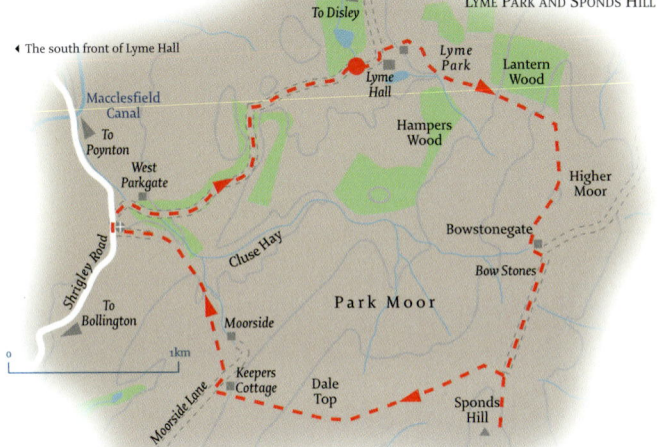

◀ The south front of Lyme Hall

by the Legh family in the 16th century as boundary markers, lie a little off to the left. The onward route turns right along the delightful walled lane for the next 600m with open views, especially ahead to Sponds Hill. The lane dips, then rises to a point where the wall veers off to the right. Here, you can carry on for 300m to the highest point of Sponds Hill, though its triangulation point lies to the west of the track in private land.

The onward route turns right with the wall, marking the southern boundary of Park Moor, and soon descends into a dip before rising to the high point of Dale Top. Here, the footpath leaves the boundary wall and, from a point 50m to the south, continues its route westwards across a stile and downhill alongside another less well-maintained wall. This meets Moorside Lane in 600m at Keepers Cottage.

Turn right up the rough lane for just 100m, before taking the footpath off left,

which heads diagonally across the moorland field. Soon after passing the house of Moorside away to the right, you start to descend again beside a wall on the right, at which point marker posts guide you a little left, down into a scrubby dell and across a stream. Once out of the dell, the wall shows the way again, down two fields to a gate by the house of Lark Hill. The lane beyond leads down past cottages to a Methodist Chapel and Shrigley Road.

At this point, ensure you turn sharp right, forking off Shrigley Road and down a narrow lane to the bridge over the stream at West Parkgate. Here, a right turn through the gate takes you back into Lyme Park (the gate is locked at 8.30pm in summer), where a track beside the stream heads up through a wooded dell for just over 1km to a gate onto the car park at The Knott. From here, a driveway leads you through the open parkland for the final 600m back down to the main car park.

Goyt Valley and Shining Tor

Distance 17km **Time** 5 hours
Terrain byways and field paths; open
moorland ridges with total ascent of 500m
Map OS Explorer OL24 **Access** train to
Whaley Bridge, bus from Whaley Bridge

**A walk of contrasts, from woodland and
waterside to open moorland views from
the highest point in Cheshire.**

The Goyt Valley has been inhabited
since Neolithic times but the 20th century
saw rapid changes from working farmland
to a landscape of reservoirs and forestry.
For the supply of water – aptly this is the
meaning of the Anglo-Saxon *gota* –
Fernilee was flooded in 1938 and Errwood
in 1967. This saw the demolition of many
of the valley's farms and homes. Even the
Victorian mansion of Errwood Hall did
not survive. Yet today the valley is so
popular a traffic management scheme,
introduced in 1970, restricts access on
summer Sundays and Bank Holidays.

From the lay-by on the A5004 Buxton
Road, 1.5km south of Whaley Bridge
(GR008798), head down the byway into
woodland above the River Goyt and once
round the left-hand bend take the
footpath into Shallcross Wood. For the
next 2km this undulates through the
trees before crossing a series of riverside
meadows beside the River Goyt. At the
end of the fourth field you re-enter
woodland and pass an industrial building
before picking up a tarmac lane which
zigzags steeply up to Fernilee Reservoir.

Continue for 1.7km along the disused
railway track on the reservoir's east side.
Just before the end of the reservoir, bear
left up the steep access road to Errwood
Reservoir dam. The route heads across
this before bearing left up to a T-junction.
Here, a left turn takes you along the
reservoir's west side for 900m, over
Shooter's Clough Bridge to Errwood Hall
Car Park and picnic area near the southern

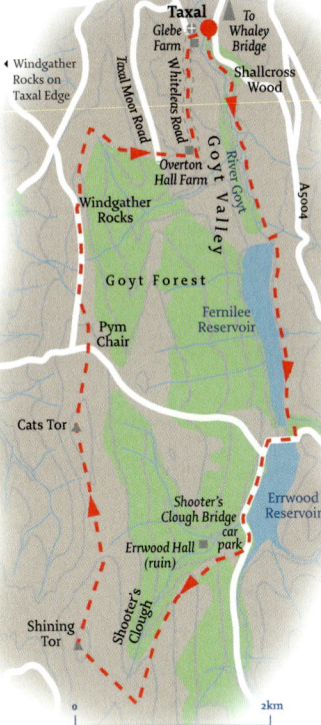

Windgather
Rocks on
Taxal Edge

Taxal
Glebe
Farm

To
Whaley
Bridge

Shallcross
Wood

Taxal Moor Road

Whiteleas Road

River Goyt

Goyt Valley

Overton
Hall Farm

A5004

Windgather
Rocks

Goyt Forest

Fernilee
Reservoir

Pym
Chair

Cats Tor

Shooter's
Clough Bridge

Errwood
Reservoir

car
park

Errwood Hall
(ruin)

Shining
Tor

Shooter's Clough

0   2km

broad ridge for another 1.2km to its high point at a wall and path junction. Now turn right (SP Shining Tor) and head northwestwards across the dip before the final climb to Shining Tor, the highest point in Cheshire.

The next 5km follows some of the finest moorland ridge-walking in the Peak District. Initially descend NNE on paving slabs to a flatter section before the rise to Cats Tor. From here a peaty path drops to Pym Chair and the moorland road down to Errwood. This is the old packhorse route and a favourite haunt of the highwayman Pym, a suitable place to ambush packhorse trains led by jaggers carrying salt from the brine pits of Cheshire.

Cross the road and continue northwards over the moorland for 450m before rejoining the road for 1km to a bend. A footpath now takes you over the top of Windgather Rocks before descending Taxal Edge alongside a field-wall for 500m to farm buildings.

Here, turn right onto a footpath along the bottom of this field, switch to the left side of the fence and crest the small ridge ahead. Descend the moorland, over Taxal Moor Road, to reach Overton Hall Farm. Past the farm buildings, turn left to follow the rough lane of Whiteleas Road for 1.2km to Taxal. Just before St James' Church and its memorials to the Jodrell family, turn right onto a byway down across the River Goyt and fork left up to the lay-by.

end of the reservoir. You can explore the ruins of the hall by following the Forestry Commission woodland walk and plaques.

The nature of the walk now changes with an initial ascent of 250m. Look out for a footpath to the right (SP Stakeside) uphill through trees, then continue up a grassy slope between plantations to a moorland wall. Bear left beside the wall (SP Cat and Fiddle) – ignore the path to Shooter's Clough – and continue up the

43

Tegg's Nose Country Park

Distance 4km **Time** 1 hour 30
Terrain lanes and paths with a moderate
climb **Map** OS Explorer OL24 **Access** bus
from Macclesfield stops at Langley, 500m
from the start

**This short but, in places, steep route
provides a perfect stroll, with plenty to
catch the eye along the way.**

Tegg's Nose Country Park is now a
popular place for walking, cycling, fishing
and even sledging, though reminders of
its industrial past as a quarry have been
preserved, with examples of the
equipment that was used to quarry the
sandstone rock here, blocks of which were
destined, among other places, for the
pavements of nearby Macclesfield.

The walk starts from Tegg's Nose
Country Park's lower car park on the
north side of Teggsnose Reservoir, which
lies 500m northeast of the village of
Langley. Starting here has the advantage
of completing the uphill section in the
first half of the walk, but a start from the
upper, and larger, car park on Buxton Old
Road to the north is possible, or may be
necessary at busy periods. To reach the
lower car park from the centre of Langley
head up Main Road and then turn left
along Holehouse Lane to the reservoir.

From the lower car park walk back
across the dam and turn left onto the
bridleway along the reservoir's south side.
The two reservoirs here were used to
regulate the water supply to factories in
Langley, Bottoms Reservoir being built in
1850 and the smaller Teggsnose Reservoir
constructed slightly later in 1871. At the
second stream cross the stepping stones

and keep ahead up some shallow steps in the main track (ignore the path off to the left) and in another 400m reach a lane junction by Clough House.

Branch left up the lane for 200m, after which you should turn left up the concessionary bridleway of Saddlers Way. Initially cobbled, it rises steeply up through a gate and continues up to the visitor centre and the upper car park.

Walk through the upper car park to the road, where you should turn left (SP Country Park) onto the Gritstone Trail, initially alongside Buxton Old Road, and then for another 300m to a gate. Here, turn left up some steps with the Gritstone Trail, which now heads south past Tegg's Nose Quarry, with its wall, a steep pit and some old quarrying machines, including a rockcrusher and a swingsaw, as well as a number of information boards which explain the history of the place.

Continue past the quarry to a viewpoint and topograph. The path curves right, round the head of Tegg's Nose to a gate, beyond which the main path keeps right for a little way before dropping left and descending across the open parkland. Keep on down through the woodland to a lower gate, where steps will lead you down to the lower car park.

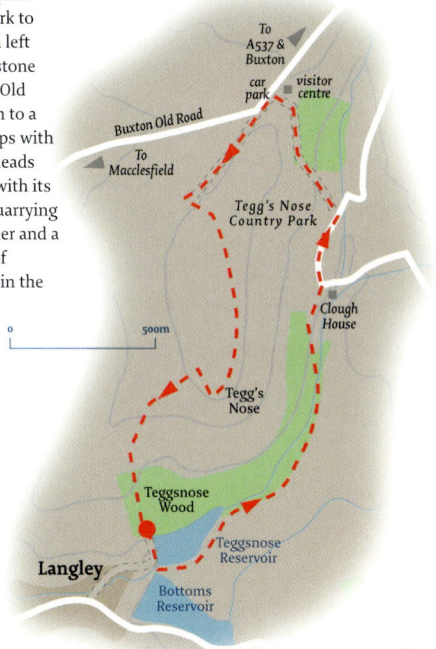

Macclesfield Forest and Shutlingsloe

Distance 10km **Time** 3 hours 30
Terrain lanes, forest tracks and open
moorland (with ascent of 450m)
Map OS Explorer OL24 **Access** no public
transport to the start

**A moorland and mountain outing
with far-reaching views.**

If you want to indulge in some peak-
bagging then Shutlingsloe has to be on
the list. It is apparently known by some as
the Staffordshire Matterhorn. Whether
firmly tongue-in-cheek or self-
deprecatory, first impressions do not give
much credence to the comparison with
the mountainous pyramid of rock
towering nearly nine times the height
above Zermatt. However, every hill reveals
a little more of itself the more you
discover of it and Shutlingsloe in certain
conditions can feel bigger and higher
than its modest 506m would suggest.

From the car park on the south side of
Trentabank Reservoir (GR961711) walk
eastwards past the visitor centre building,
parallel with the road, for 100m to a bike
squeeze gate. Here, turn right and follow
the waymarked red route posts which
wend and climb their way southwards
towards Shutlingsloe, rising up through
the forest for 1.25km until you reach a
gate at the southern edge of the trees.
Continue along the track for another
250m before turning right onto a footpath
which leads up to a gate onto the open
moorland of Piggford Moor.

From here a flagged path heads
southeastwards up over Shutlingsloe's
northwest shoulder to a cross-paths at a
wall after 600m. Turn right for the steep
pull up to the triangulation point. To
continue, start down the south ridge to
pick up a path which curves left down the
hill's southeastern flank for 750m to reach

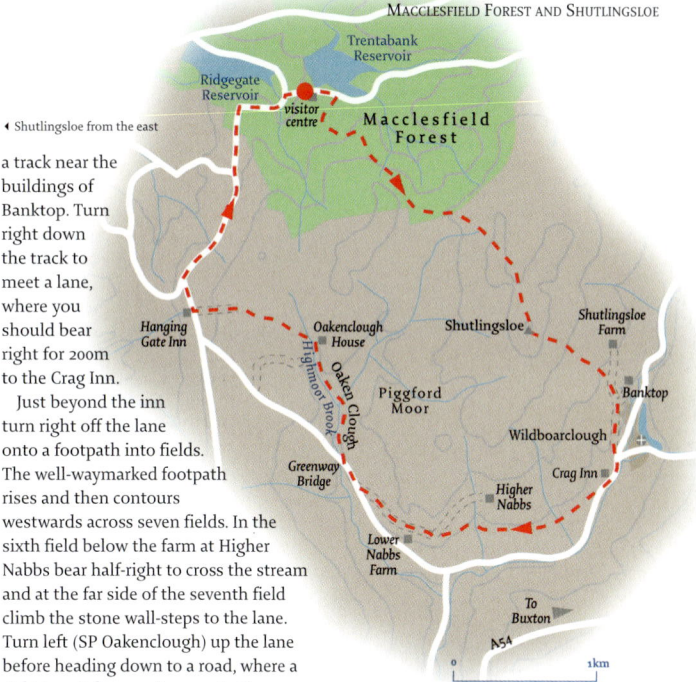

◄ Shutlingsloe from the east

Trentabank Reservoir

Ridgegate Reservoir

visitor centre

Macclesfield Forest

Hanging Gate Inn

Oakenclough House

Shutlingsloe

Shutlingsloe Farm

Highmoor Brook

Oaken Clough

Piggford Moor

Banktop

Wildboarclough

Greenway Bridge

Crag Inn

Higher Nabbs

Lower Nabbs Farm

To Buxton

A54

0   1km

a track near the buildings of Banktop. Turn right down the track to meet a lane, where you should bear right for 200m to the Crag Inn.

Just beyond the inn turn right off the lane onto a footpath into fields. The well-waymarked footpath rises and then contours westwards across seven fields. In the sixth field below the farm at Higher Nabbs bear half-right to cross the stream and at the far side of the seventh field climb the stone wall-steps to the lane. Turn left (SP Oakenclough) up the lane before heading down to a road, where a right turn takes you in 300m to Greenway Bridge over Highmoor Brook.

Here, turn right and follow the footpath alongside the brook for 350m to a footbridge, where you should bear left across it and follow the grassy path up the side of Oaken Clough to a junction with a track leading to Oakenclough House. Across the track, take the footpath up beside the wall and then continue WNW across open moorland for 150m to a boggy section by a peaty pool, before veering west and, after 100m, picking up the line of a wall to take you over the brow of the

hill. Just down from the brow, you'll need to dogleg right, then left to descend the old Roman salt lane down to the road and the Hanging Gate Inn.

Here, turn right down this quiet road for 200m, with good views left to Croker Hill and Sutton Common, and at the bend bear right to continue northwards down a twisting lane for 1.25km to a sharp right bend. At this point, you can either continue to follow the lane or take the signed forestry track on the right back to Trentabank Reservoir.

47

Chelmorton and Wye Dale

Distance 9km **Time** 2 hours 30
Terrain tracks, fields and marked trails
with one steep descent
Map OS Explorer OL24 **Access** bus
from Buxton and Sheffield

**Stride out from high on the limestone
plateau down into the gorge of the River
Wye, and return past Five Wells
Chambered Tomb.**

Chelmorton is one of the highest
villages in the Peak District, standing at
nearly 400m above sea level. There are a
number of plaques around the village to
help interpret the linear layout of the
medieval strip fields, still visible in outline
either side of the main street. Along this
ran a series of interconnected troughs fed
by the spring of the Illy-Willy-Water below
Chelmorton Low. Here also is the medieval
Church of St John the Baptist with its
unusual weather vane of a gilded locust,
glinting if the sun is out.

From the top end of the village of
Chelmorton, just below the church and
the Church Inn, take the bridleway off to
the left. This pleasant track runs past the
Old Vicarage and Shepley Farm, with good
views right to the slopes of Chelmorton
Low and left over the rectilinear pattern of
fields surrounding the village.

Across the A5270, avoid the footpath
straight ahead and instead dogleg left to
follow the bridleway along Caxterway
Lane (SP Burrs Farm). After 500m the track
curves north and descends to a gate. Bear
right over the wall onto a footpath which
crosses diagonally down the field to a
stile perched high above Topley Pike
Quarry. The next section involves a short
but steep descent into Wye Dale, a stark
contrast to the easy walking so far. Bear a
little to the left before heading back to the
right where you can pick up a path which
traverses below the topmost limestone
outcrop and then zigzags down the nose
of the short ridge to a gate at the bottom.
Here, you can detour up the side valley to
the right for 200m to explore the Churn
Hole. The onward route heads left down

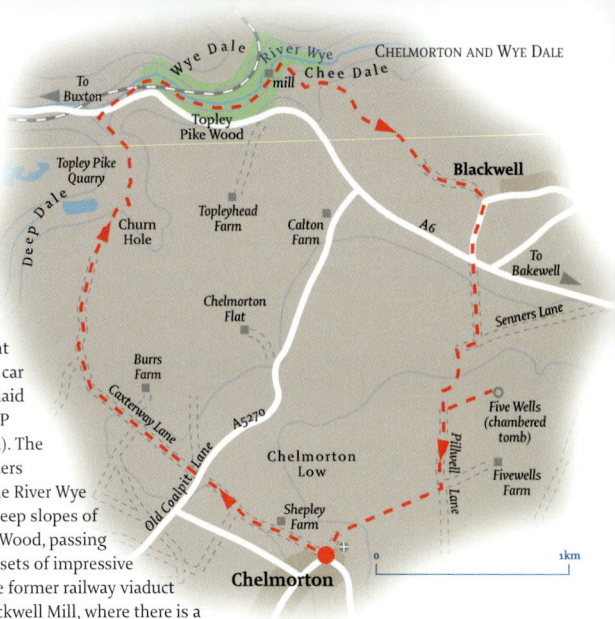

the fence and past the quarry entrance to the A6.

Across the A6, turn right through the car park onto a laid bridleway (SP Monsal Trail). The track meanders alongside the River Wye below the steep slopes of Topley Pike Wood, passing under three sets of impressive arches of the former railway viaduct to reach Blackwell Mill, where there is a snack bar and cycle hire open in high season – a good place to pause for a rest or a picnic.

The route turns right up to and across the Monsal Trail onto the Pennine Bridleway which heads up the side valley. After 100m look out for a footpath off left (SP Blackwell), which zigzags up through the limestone outcrops and up a short ridge to a fence, with good views down into Chee Dale. The route now heads up a series of fields – in the third one climb to the left – to rejoin the Pennine Bridleway. Follow this waymarked route for the next 2km, bearing right onto the road at the hamlet of Blackwell, across the A6 again and steeply up Pillwell Lane to the top of the escarpment.

Here, a concession path leads left over fields for 300m to Five Wells Chambered Tomb, dated to the Neolithic period some 5000 years ago. Common to the Peak District but not elsewhere, the burial chambers are covered by a round barrow. Originally the mound would have been higher, but most of the surface was robbed of its stone in the 18th century. Inside excavations revealed the remains of more than a dozen skeletons, along with pottery, arrowheads and burnt bones.

Carry on over the rise for 400m to the start of the tarmac road and then take the grassy bridleway, signed for Chelmorton, to the right. This soon drops between widely-spaced stone walls past the Illy-Willy-Water spring and back to the church.

◄ Five Wells Chambered Tomb

Upper Dove Hills

Distance 7km **Time** 3 hours
Terrain lanes, fields, tracks, with 350m of
ascent, steep and exposed at times
Map OS Explorer OL24 **Access** no public
transport to the start

**Lace up your boots for one of the best
mini-mountaineering routes in the
White Peak.**

The Peak District does not offer many
longer routes where the use of hands or a
head for heights are necessary. But these
enticing steep-sided limestone hills at the
head of the Upper Dove Valley are not to
be underestimated and in wintry
conditions the precipitous slopes can be
quite an undertaking. They owe their
shape to their origin 300 million years ago
as coral reefs in a shallow sea. Since then
ice, wind and rain have eroded them into
the dragon's back edge of Chrome Hill

(pronounced 'kroom') and Parkhouse
Hill's shark's fin ridge.

From the centre of the village of
Hollinsclough near the Methodist Chapel
head down the lane past the primary
school. In 400m just before the right-hand
bend, bear left onto a track which heads
past an old stone barn. Chrome and
Parkhouse Hills are now clearly seen
towering ahead. In 350m take the right
fork in the track (SP Glutton Bridge)
alongside a stream, over a footbridge and
up to the road.

Here, a short dogleg right along the
road brings you to a faint footpath off left
which allows you to contour around the
south side of Parkhouse Hill for 300m to a
wall. Turn left uphill alongside the wall as
it snakes its way for 200m round to the
start of the hill's eastern ridge. This grassy
ridge makes for a very steep and

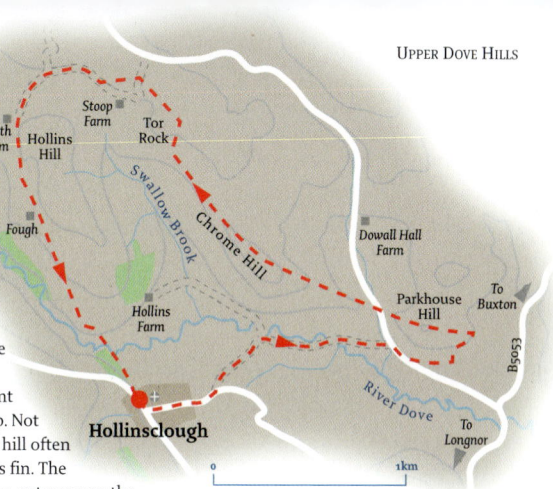

exhilarating ascent of 170m and you'll need a good head for heights as the feeling of exposure is considerable, though the gradient eases off higher up. Not for nothing is this hill often likened to a shark's fin. The grass and limestone outcrops on the descent of the west ridge make for some thoughtful manoeuvres, especially in the wet. The easiest line is to pass to the right of the first pinnacle and then avoid the last pinnacles on the ridge, either by exiting sharp right to easier grassy slopes or by descending a loose path on the left down to the road. If conditions or disposition merit it, this hill can be omitted altogether and the road followed to the ridge up Chrome Hill.

Head for the stile at the bottom of the southeast ridge of Chrome Hill, from where a signed 'concession path' leads you in 300m up to the start of Access Land again. Here the ridge steepens. Though it is less exposed than Parkhouse Hill, the 150m ascent is nonetheless every bit as satisfying and the views are, if possible, even better. The descent follows the northwest ridge over several limestone bimples to a gate in the wall at the edge of Access Land.

A concession path now leads you over two fields before zigzagging sharply right uphill and then left along higher ground above Stoop Farm. At the driveway to the farm, take the path ahead (SP Booth Farm) over four fields and down to the road, where a left turn leads you in 250m up to the farm and Access Land at the northwestern end of Hollins Hill.

Here, the energetic may want to attempt the rough traverse of Hollins Hill itself, but for a gentler walk fork left onto the bridleway which descends pleasantly along the south side of the hill, in 500m passing the house at Fough and in another 500m a concession path on the left to the southern end of Hollins Hill. Below this point, the way narrows and you'll need to drop down over sometimes boggy ground to a footbridge over the stream before climbing the far side up to the road. Here, a left turn downhill takes you back into Hollinsclough.

◄ Chrome Hill from above Stoop Farm

Hitter Hill and High Wheeldon

Distance 4km **Time** 1 hour 30
Terrain lanes, fields and tracks, one very
steep ascent with easier alternative
Map OS Explorer OL24 **Access** bus to Earl
Sterndale from Ashbourne and Buxton

**Get your lungs working with a short but
strenuous walk in the Upper Dove Valley.**

These steep-sided limestone hills are
two further ancient reef knolls in the
Upper Dove Valley and it would be
entirely feasible to combine their ascent
with Parkhouse and Chrome Hills for a
longer outing.

From the centre of Earl Sterndale by the
church take the footpath which heads
from the back of The Quiet Woman pub.
The unusual headless sign outside reveals
the macabre origins of the inn's
perplexing name; in one version of the
legend to which the name refers the
landlady was relieved of her head during
an argument with her husband. Walk to

the right of the pub buildings and then
immediately left into fields (ignore the
footpath straight on which leads to
Hollinsclough). Follow the wall up two
fields to the edge of Access Land, from
where you can detour to the right to the
very top of Hitter Hill and the view to the
Upper Dove Hills. The footpath hugs the
wall and descends to the edge of Access
Land again, before continuing across the
top of the field ahead. After just 50m,
before the wall kinks away to the left, the
footpath drops to the right on a
descending traverse to a gate and across
the next field to a house and byway.

Turn left along the byway which traces a
route across the top of fields for 400m to
the buildings of Underhill. Past the
cowsheds you continue along the lane
which, after another 250m, bends left at
the junction with Green Lane and heads
up to the road to Crowdicote. Here, you

◀ The steep slopes of High Wheeldon from Earl Sterndale

have a choice of routes for the ascent of High Wheeldon.

For the shorter but more challenging option, dogleg left along the road, then right over the stile into Access Land. From here, you head in an easterly direction straight up the unremittingly steep grassy slope where there is a considerable sense of exposure though no real difficulty. However, a slip here could have nasty consequences. The gradient finally eases off after an ascent of 150m and you can take in the view from the triangulation point, with its Second World War memorial plaque to the men of Derbyshire and Staffordshire. For the longer but easier way up, turn left up the road and, at Aldery Cliff, turn right and use the descent route described below but in reverse.

The hill is also a significant archaeological site. Just below the summit on the northern slopes lies Fox Hole Cave. The cave consists of a passage and several chambers and in excavations carried out in the 20th century remains were found dating back to Palaeolithic times. Flint artefacts and animal remains were found. In addition, bones and antlers made into spearpoints have been radiocarbon-dated to 10,000BC and attest to some of the earliest human habitation in the region.

To descend off High Wheeldon, follow the narrow path for 200m down the northeastern side to a wall, where a left turn alongside the wall takes you round the north side of the hill to the road opposite Aldery Cliff. It's now a simple matter of turning right and following the pleasant road for 1km back up into Earl Sterndale.

Gradbach and Lud's Church

Distance 7.5km **Time** 2 hours 30 (with
detour to Lud's Church) **Terrain** lanes,
woodland and open moorland
Map OS Explorer OL24 **Access** no public
transport to the start

**This walk combines peaceful woodland, a
grassy ridge and the famous landslip
chasm of Lud's Church.**

The arguments surrounding the name
of Lud's Church reveal a little of the
mystery of the place. Some see an
etymological connection with the
Lollards, those 14th-century religious
followers of John Wycliff who espoused
the denial of transubstantiation in the
mass and a return for the church to
apostolic poverty and purity, though their
abhorrence of shrines casts some doubt
on this theory. Others make a close
topographical reading of the medieval
poem *Sir Gawain and the Green Knight* and

link the place to the Green Chapel, to
which Gawain must return at New Year to
face the headless Green Knight. It may be
that all this simply ties in with the ageless
pagan myth of the Green Man, harbinger
of spring and regeneration, seen on old
churches, over doorways and even on pub
signs. How apt that the Green Man is
above all an enigma, who may now be
reemerging as a symbol of how to
reconnect with nature.

The walk starts from the car park 500m
east of Gradbach Mill (GR998662), situated
off the minor road linking the A54 at
Allgreave and the A53 at Flash – after 3km
on either approach take the lane to
Gradbach for 300m, where you'll find the
car park on the right.

From the car park turn right to continue
gently uphill along the lane with the River
Dane down to the right. After 250m a right
turn takes you down the driveway to

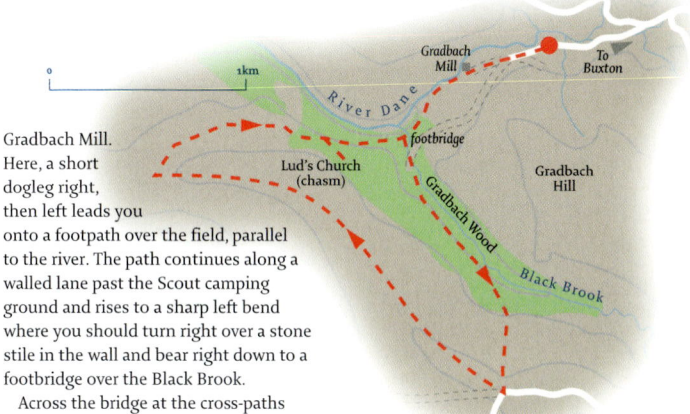

Gradbach Mill.
Here, a short
dogleg right,
then left leads you
onto a footpath over the field, parallel
to the river. The path continues along a
walled lane past the Scout camping
ground and rises to a sharp left bend
where you should turn right over a stone
stile in the wall and bear right down to a
footbridge over the Black Brook.

Across the bridge at the cross-paths
turn left (SP The Roaches) into woodland,
initially beside the brook but then,
beyond the old ford, the path heads up
through the oak trees before descending
to meet a path up from the left. Here,
continue uphill to a path junction with a
line of beech trees (ignore the right turn
to Lud's Church) and keep ahead across
the stream to the southern edge of the
wood and out onto the bracken- and
heather-covered moorland up to the
path's high point by a bend in the road.

The character of the route now changes
as it heads right (SP Lud's Church &
Swythamley) along the crest of the ridge,
with views back towards The Roaches and
ahead the pointed top of Shutlingsloe,
with the town of Leek away to the south.
The ridge makes for delightful walking
over undulating and grassy ground and
past rocky outcrops, heading northwest
for 1.5km over two high points on this
section of ridge (after the first high point
ignore a path off right to Lud's Church).

From the second high point you should
stay on the crest for the next 1km as you
veer westwards and descend to a path
junction at the edge of Access Land.

Now turn right and head gently
downhill for 750m into mixed woodland.
In another 100m the path forks at a
junction by a rocky tor on the left. The left
branch heads back to Gradbach, but you
can explore Lud's Church by detouring
right for 200m where you'll find the lower
entrance to the chasm on the right of the
path. You can walk right through the
chasm itself, either retracing your steps to
the lower entrance or heading up to the
top end where you can circle back down to
the left through the woodland.

Retrace your steps to the path junction
and turn right onto the path back to
Gradbach. This descends for another
500m, where a fingerpost for Gradbach
points the way down to the footbridge
over the Black Brook. From here, follow
the outward route back to the car park.

Hen Cloud and The Roaches

Distance 11.5km **Time** 4 hours
Terrain lanes, fields, moorland slopes and
edges with 400m of ascent, steep in
places **Map** OS Explorer OL24
Access no public transport to the start

**A longer approach to The Roaches, one of
the most popular destinations in the
Peak for walkers and climbers.**

This route avoids the shorter option of
the road up from Upper Hulme and
instead winds its way up from the village
of Meerbrook over fields to the north of
Tittesworth Reservoir before climbing the
well-known slopes.

From the centre of Meerbrook, 2km
west of the A53, by the Lazy Trout pub,
head north for 200m along the lane bound
for Roche Grange. After the bend turn
right onto a footpath down the drive to
Lower Lee Farm, past a row of cottages
and into fields beyond, following the
signed Staffordshire Moorlands Walk
(SMW) with a view of Hen Cloud and
The Roaches ahead.

The route is well-marked and heads
north across a series of fields – at the end
of the fourth field turn right on a track
which leads in 200m to the buildings of
Frith Bottom. Here, you should turn right
into fields once more. In the first field
beyond the house curve left and use the
series of small footbridges and
boardwalks to negotiate the boggy
sections. Then cross over the second field
to a footbridge over a stream, where a left
turn leads you northeastwards up past a
stone barn and over a second field. Here
you leave the SMW, which bears off right,
and continue up three more fields to the
farm buildings at Windygates – in this
section the gap between Hen Cloud and
The Roaches serves as a handy pointer.
Squeeze to the left of the cowsheds,
before taking the track in front of the
farmhouse up to the road.

The route doglegs right for 150m
along the road, then left along
the track to The Roaches
House and soon
curves right

below the crags of Hen Cloud.
Just before the cattle grid and
gate to the house, turn left off
the track and pick your way up
through the beech trees and
below a steep crag, then circle
more steeply up to the left to
reach a path leading through
the heather to the top of Hen
Cloud. This gives a good
view northeast to Ramshaw
Rocks and northwest to
the line of The Roaches.

To continue, descend
NNW into the dip to a gate
and across a field to the
start of The Roaches.
To gain the top of the
escarpment you can
follow a number of paths
up through the climbers'
crags, but the main one for walkers
heads to the right before curving back to
the left, reaching Doxey Pool after 700m
and then after a further 1.1km the
triangulation pillar and the high point of
the ridge. From here, the route descends
for 750m to a lane.

The return route turns left down the
lane, after 900m forking right for
Meerbrook and descending more steeply
down through the houses of Roche
Grange. At the right bend beyond, either
carry on along the lane for a further 2.5km
or, if conditions underfoot are dry, keep
ahead over three fields to Roach Side

Farm; once past the house turn right
across a small field, before bearing right
and following the waymarks southwards
down a series of four more fields to meet
the lane again.

From here, head round the bend in the
lane and in 30m look out for a footpath
off to the left. Cross a small field and
branch right down two larger fields to a
stream, before heading up a fourth to its
far left corner, then left across a fifth field
to meet the track to Frith Bottom once
more. From here, you can retrace the
outward route back to Meerbrook.

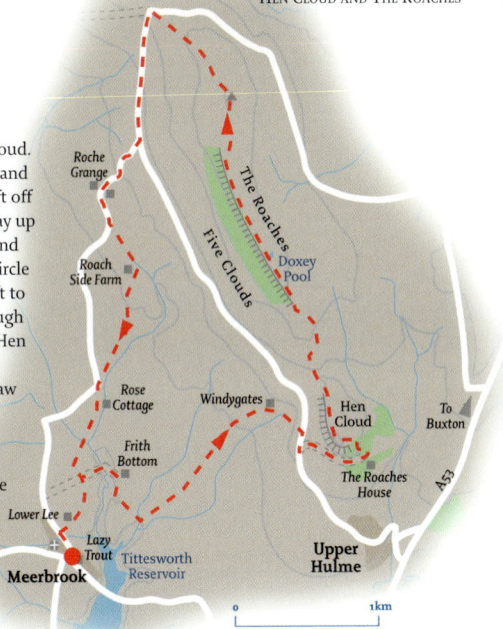

◂ Nearing the high point on The Roaches

57

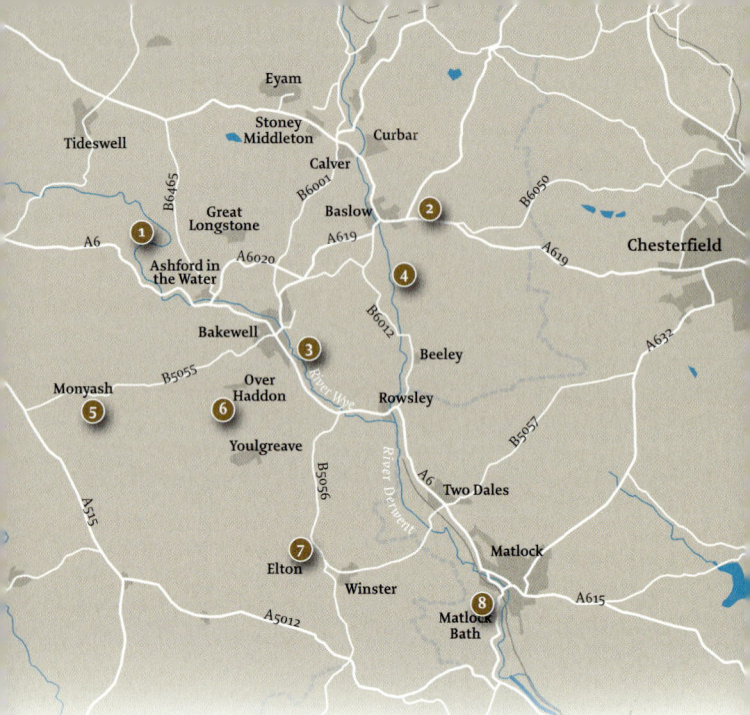

The area stretching from Bakewell to Matlock contains some of the most enjoyable walking the Peak District has to offer. Bakewell itself is the only market town within the Peak District National Park and is still very much a thriving centre. Close by are two of the Peak's most famous country houses, Haddon Hall, home of the Duke of Rutland on the River Wye, and Chatsworth House, seat of the Devonshires on the River Derwent. North of the town the Monsal Viaduct cuts across Wye Dale, and high on Birchen Edge above Baslow can be found a monument to Admiral Nelson, with his three 'ships' hard by.

Lathkill Dale lies to the southwest and forms part of a National Nature Reserve of Derbyshire dales. Once pockmarked with leadmines the dale's natural habitat has been largely restored. On the approach to Matlock, gritstone outcrops overlie the limestone again and the town, or rather the series of five towns, spreads itself along the River Derwent. The town still attracts its fair share of tourists, as it has done for several hundred years now.

Paine's Bridge at Chatsworth ▸

Bakewell and the East

Monsal Head

Distance 9km **Time** 2 hours 30
Terrain old railway track, field and
riverside paths, byways, with one steep
ascent **Map** OS Explorer OL24 **Access** bus
from Bakewell and Castleton

**Monsal Head is one of the best known
spots in the Peak District and the view
down into Wye Dale is still as dramatic
as it ever was.**

The first part of the route follows the
Monsal Trail, which heads along the
disused line of the Midland Railway. The
viaduct was built in 1863 and was to some
a controversial construction, cutting
through the heart of the Wye Valley. It has
now become an iconic feature, though the
tracks are long gone and trains run no
more. From the 18th century the waters of
the River Wye were used to power the
cottonmills at Cressbrook and Litton Mill.
Many of the former industrial buildings
have now been converted to residential
use. On the route, there are various
information boards which help to picture
the history of the place.

From the viewpoint at Monsal Head
descend steps on the right to Monsal
Viaduct, turning left after 75m down to
the line of the former Midland Railway,
which now carries the Monsal Trail.
A right turn takes you over the impressive
viaduct and on through Upperdale for the
next 1.5km to the start of Cressbrook
Tunnel. Here, bear right off the Monsal
Trail onto a narrower concession path

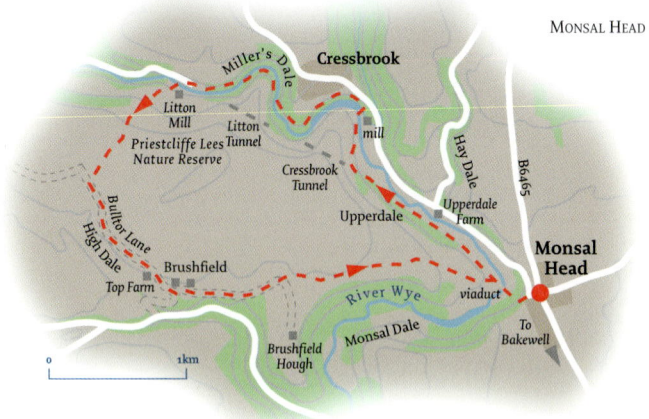

across the grassy slope ahead and down to the River Wye, with a good view to Cressbrook Mill on the opposite bank.

After crossing the footbridge over the river by the weir, fork left onto a riverside path beneath the cliffs. (The path here is prone to flooding – if so, you have two options: either retrace your steps to Cressbrook Tunnel and head through it to Litton or stay on this bank and take the right fork to Cressbrook. Head past the former mill to the road, then turn sharp left uphill and, once past Rock House, take the concession path on the left through woodland and back down to the river.) The riverside route makes for pleasant walking up the meandering gorge of Water-cum-Jolly Dale and Miller's Dale to the houses and former factory buildings at Litton. Here, bear right to pass up between houses to the road and, after another 30m, look out for a footpath off to the left (SP Monsal Trail).

You now recross the River Wye and zigzag up through woodland to the Monsal Trail, where a dogleg right takes you to some steps up to the left just before the bridge. At the top, turn left onto a path which heads fairly steeply up into the nature reserve of Priestcliffe Lees, over two fields before levelling off between stone walls. In another 100m, cross the wall on the left and head down the field beyond to Bulltor Lane.

Here, a left turn takes you for the next 1.2km along this old undulating lane above High Dale and down past the farm buildings at Brushfield. Just beyond Middle Farm, look out for a left turn which heads past Lower Farm cottages. Go through the gate and after 700m, at the fork in the track to Brushfield Hough, keep left for Upperdale. The track keeps on uphill and across fields before starting the descent, gentle at first with good views across Monsal Dale to the prominent top of Fin Cop and then more steeply to bring you down once more to Upperdale and the Monsal Viaduct.

◀ The view from Monsal Head to its viaduct and Wye Dale

Birchen Edge and Nelson's Monument

Distance 2km **Time** 45 minutes
Terrain woodland, bracken and crag-top
paths **Map** OS Explorer OL24 **Access** bus
from Baslow and Chesterfield

A short but energetic stroll with some
great views, just right for a clear evening.
It makes a good option for a picnic too,
though be aware that there are steep
drops to watch out for.

The walk starts from Birchen Edge
car park, which is located just off the
A619, 3km east of Baslow, next to The
Robin Hood Inn. Head up the B6050 for
50m and take the path off left up to

a gate, continuing beyond up into
woodland. In 200m, at a fork in the
path by a large boulder, turn right for
a short but steep pull up to the top of
Birchen Edge.

Here, you should turn left to follow
the twisting path up through the heather
and bracken, with an increasingly steep
drop on the left, to reach Nelson's
Monument, thought to have been funded
and erected by the Baslow businessman
John Brightman in 1810 to honour the
admiral and celebrate the victory at the
Battle of Trafalgar in 1805, though Nelson's
name does not actually appear on the

monument. On the right are the rocks known as the Three Ships, with the names of the warships *Victory*, *Defiance* and *Royal Soverin* carved into the stone on their 'prows'. Nelson's Column in Trafalgar Square was erected in 1840 but Brightman's was not the first monument to Nelson, being preceded by ones in Glasgow (1806), Edinburgh and Portsmouth (1807) and Montreal, Birmingham and Hereford (1809). Though idealised after his death as a seafaring hero, Nelson was against the abolition of slavery and exerted his influence to thwart campaigners' efforts to end Britain's part in the transatlantic slave trade.

What perhaps makes Birchen particular is that climbers also use the area for topping out, though they are forbidden to belay off the monument itself, and the majority of routes here have names of a nautical nature, such as Portside, The Gangplank, Horatio's Horror, Moby Dick, Mayday and even The Kraken – graded Extreme it's certainly a monstrous climb.

The route continues for 150m to the triangulation point, with a good view northwards to Curbar and Froggatt Edges. To descend, take the path just beyond the triangulation point down the escarpment, forking left at the base and then left again onto the lower path. This takes you back along the base of the climbing crags, which can be a real suntrap, and then back down to the gate above the B6050 and the car park at the start.

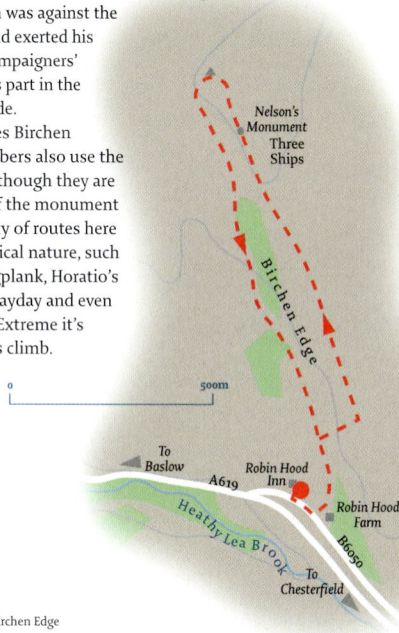

◀ Nelson's Monument atop Birchen Edge

Bakewell and Manners Wood

Distance 8km **Time** 2 hours 15
Terrain riverside paths and woodland
tracks **Map** OS Explorer OL24 **Access** bus
from Sheffield, Matlock and Buxton

**A delightful riverside and woodland
walk, with the option of a visit to the
historic manor house of Haddon Hall.**

Known for its famous pudding and
tart, the busy market town of Bakewell
is also the administrative centre of the
national park and is ideally positioned at
a crossing point of the River Wye. The
five-arched bridge was built in the 13th
century and widened in the 19th.

If you come in late June you can see the
fascinating Derbyshire tradition of well-
dressing here. Believed to have been
brought to the area by the Romans or
Celts to give thanks for the area's
freshwater springs, the ancient tradition
sees volunteers create intricate mosaics
out of clay, leaves, petals, moss and other
natural materials which are then
positioned above their local well.

The walk itself passes close to the
fortified medieval manor house of
Haddon Hall, which has a romantic tale of
the elopement of John Manners, whose
monument can be seen in the town's
Church of All Saints.

From Bridge Street in the centre of
Bakewell head along Market Street and
over the River Wye to Smith's Island car
park. At the far end, cross Mill Leat Bridge
and head past the modern Agricultural

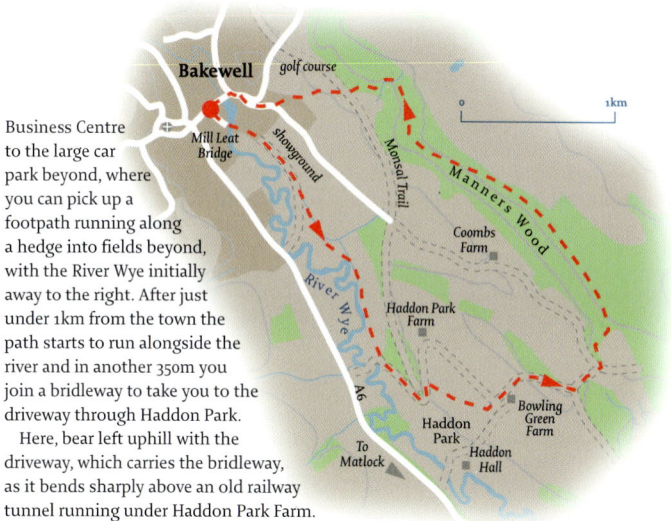

Business Centre to the large car park beyond, where you can pick up a footpath running along a hedge into fields beyond, with the River Wye initially away to the right. After just under 1km from the town the path starts to run alongside the river and in another 350m you join a bridleway to take you to the driveway through Haddon Park.

Here, bear left uphill with the driveway, which carries the bridleway, as it bends sharply above an old railway tunnel running under Haddon Park Farm. About 100m further on, round the next right-hand bend, stay on the bridleway as it veers sharp right off the driveway up alongside iron railings and across the bottom of three fields, with Haddon Park and Hall down to the right. Now the bridleway turns sharp left along a walled track, over a junction and uphill past the entrance to Bowling Green Farm, before curving right alongside a plantation and descending in 250m to a track junction. Keep left and head over the rise and down to another junction of tracks at the southern edge of Manners Wood, with a long view down the valley on the left to Bakewell and right to the moorland edges above the Derwent Valley.

Here, take the bridleway ahead uphill into Manners Wood (SP Chatsworth). The

way up through the predominantly oak woodland is fairly steep at first but in 300m you come to a track junction. At this point ensure you leave the bridleway and bear left onto the Haddon Estate concession path, which for the next 1km traces a gentler undulating route up through the now mixed woodland to a high point, before descending to a fork in the path. Keep left downhill on a narrower path for 400m until you reach a stream in a small gully. On its far side, a left turn takes you down to the golf course, where the path bears a little to the right, over a bridge above the Monsal Trail and down the field beyond to a gate onto a lane. Turn left down to Coombs Road, where a right turn soon takes you back to the River Wye and the centre of Bakewell.

◀ Bakewell from Castle Hill golf course

65

Chatsworth Park and Edensor

Distance 6km **Time** 1 hour 30
Terrain paths, tracks and parkland
Map OS Explorer OL24 **Access** bus from
**Matlock and Bakewell, Baslow and
Sheffield to Chatsworth Garden Centre**

**A stroll through the parkland and estate
of Chatsworth combines well with a visit
to the house and gardens.**

Chatsworth needs little by way of
introduction and is one of Europe's best
known houses, home to the Duke and
Duchess of Devonshire and handed down
through generations of the Cavendish
family. The present mansion replaced an
earlier Elizabethan house and its interior
contains an international art collection.
Its gardens extend over more than 100
acres and contain perhaps the final word
on water features. This route explores
some of the surrounding parkland and
takes in the village of Edensor,
pronounced Enza, which was originally
located between the River Derwent and
what is now the B6012. About 200 years
ago the family decided to move the whole
village to the other side of the road, and
the 6th Duke rebuilt much of the village
in Norman, Jacobean, Swiss and Italian
architectural styles. The result is unique.

The walk itself starts from Calton Lees
car park off the B6012, 1.5km south of
Chatsworth House. Head further down
the lane past Chatsworth Garden Centre,
which has a coffee shop and restaurant, to
the hamlet of Calton Lees. Follow the lane
round the right-hand bend and take the
bridleway ahead through a gate.

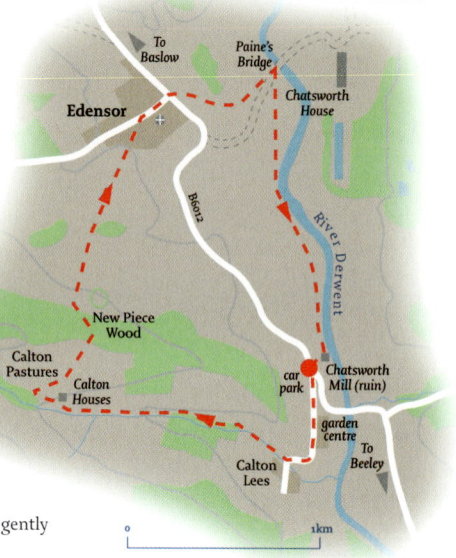

The route now leads you gently uphill in a valley beside a stream and between fields for the next 1.2km to Calton Houses. Here, zigzag up between the houses and along a walled lane to a gate. At this point the bridleway splits. Take the right fork up alongside a wall and woodland for 200m, then head over the middle of Calton Pastures and a path junction (SP Edensor and Chatsworth) to a gate into New Piece Wood. The walled bridleway descends gently to another gate on the far side.

Here, you enter the main part of Chatsworth Park itself. Initially you should bear right, still following the bridleway, down the grassy slope. After 100m at a marker post the bridleway veers off right, but the route continues onto a footpath straight ahead through a thin stand of beech and oak trees, before heading down again and passing to the left of a small plantation. From here, aim for the spire of St Peter's Church in Edensor, which you can see above the treetops. As you approach the church, just to its left look out for a metal gate up some steps, beyond which are more steps leading down into the village. Turn right through the centre of the village, passing the church and teashop on the right.

At the bottom end of the village beyond the gates cross the B6012, which runs right through the parkland, and take the footpath which curves to the right and over a rise before descending to Paine's Bridge and the main entrance to Chatsworth House. The route now turns right, across the driveway, and follows the footpath over the meadow beside the River Derwent. After 600m the footpath splits at some steps. Here, take the left fork to continue beside the river for the next 750m, passing two weirs to reach the ruin of Chatsworth Mill. At this point, bear right up to and across the road, where a left turn takes you back to the car park at Calton Lees.

◄ Chatsworth House and the River Derwent

Monyash and Upper Lathkill Dale

Distance 6km **Time** 2 hours
Terrain lanes, fields and paths, with one
steep descent and one rougher section
Map OS Explorer OL24 **Access** bus from
Bakewell and Buxton

**Lathkill Dale, stretching from Monyash to
Over Haddon and on to Alport, can
rightfully claim to be one of the most
beautiful limestone valleys. This walk
could well be combined with the route
from Over Haddon for a longer outing.**

The dale's beauty stems in part from the
semblance of seclusion given by its steep
sides and limestone cliffs, in part from the
varied mix of woodland and grassland
which occupy the valley floor. In the upper
section the rocks exposed around Ricklow
Quarry are a geologist's dream and
provide an outstanding example of a shelf
reef, formed by marine creatures some 340
million years ago. In the riverbed itself it

is also possible to see screens of tufa,
formed when calcium carbonate
precipitates in running water.

The walk starts from the centre of
Monyash at The Green, with its cross and
plinth where you can still see the holes
made by miners testing the sharpness of
their drills. Head up Rakes Road away
from the Bull's Head pub, passing pretty
Fere Mere, the only mere of four now
remaining in the village and once its
source of drinking water. After 250m at
the sharp right bend, keep left along
Derby Lane on the route of the Limestone
Way, and then left again to continue up
Milkings Lane. This delightful walled lane
rises gently between fields for 600m
before dipping slightly to the head of Fern
Dale and some grand views to Bole Hill
and beyond.

Here, ignore the concession path down
into Fern Dale ahead, but instead bear

◀ Summer flowers in Upper Lathkill Dale

right with the Limestone Way, up and across the neighbouring field. At the far side, field walls now guide you up over the rise and down to the track to One Ash Grange Farm, run by Cistercian monks in the 12th century from Roche Abbey in Yorkshire. Passing into the farmyard, keep to the left of the buildings and then between the final barns and some stone pigsties, dating from the 18th century, into the field beyond. At the far end, a gate leads to a steep descent down the limestone crags into wooded and enclosed Cales Dale. At the bottom, a fingerpost steers you left, off the Limestone Way, for Lathkill Dale.

Once over the footbridge turn left onto the path heading upstream by the River Lathkill and past the cave where the river exits from its subterranean channel, though in summer this section can run dry. There is plenty to explore here and there can be fewer more tranquil places in the Peak District, despite the dale's popularity. After 1km near the now disused Ricklow Quarry, once a source of the Ashford Marble sought after by Victorians for its satin-black finish, the dale narrows dramatically and the path squeezes its way between limestone outcrops and through boulders. However, this rougher terrain only lasts for a short while and, once past this neck, the ground opens out as the path heads over pastures for 500m to the road. Turn left to follow the grassy verge back into Monyash.

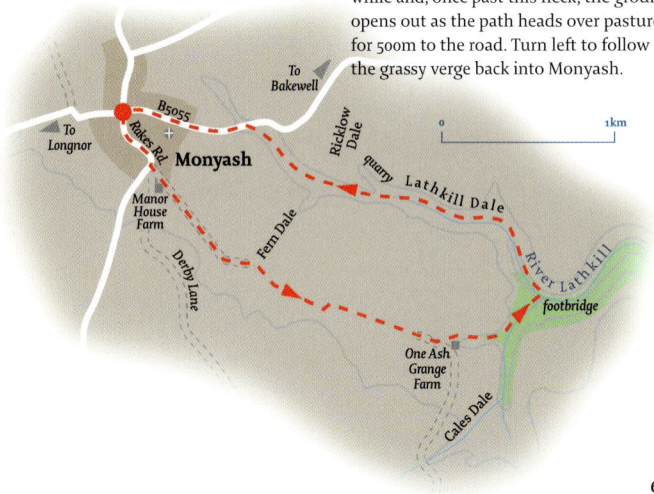

69

Over Haddon and Lathkill Dale

Distance 9km **Time** 3 hours
Terrain lanes, fields and paths, with one
steep descent **Map** OS Explorer OL24
Access bus from Bakewell

**This walk could well be combined with
the one from Monyash to appreciate
Lathkill Dale more fully.**

Over Haddon stands on the limestone
plateau just 3km southwest of Bakewell
up above Lathkill Dale, and is one of the
prettiest villages in the Peak District. This
walk crosses the dale and heads for the
high ground to the south before circling
round to allow plenty of time to explore
the length of Lathkill Dale itself.

From the west end of the village by the
Old Orchard car park, take the twisting
lane of Dale Road steeply down to the
bottom of Lathkill Dale. Across the River
Lathkill a track zigzags its way up through
the woodland to a gate. Here, bear left
into fields and over the brow to the farm
at Meadow Place Grange, a delightful
farmhouse which, despite the datestone
of 1859, was in part built in the 18th
century. The path heads through the
farmyard before bearing half-right
(SP Middleton) for the next 1km up across
three fields to Back Lane. A right turn
takes you up to the junction with Moor
Lane and its car park.

At this point the walk joins the well-
waymarked route of the Limestone Way
and bears right off the lane over four
fields to pass through Low Moor Wood,
before continuing towards the farm
buildings at Calling Low. Here, the path
skirts to the right of the farm, before
heading back left through two small
stands of woodland. On the far side, four
more fields take you downhill towards the

◄ Waymarks at Meadow Place Grange

prominent dip of Cales Dale, with the buildings of One Ash Grange visible beyond and an impressive view into Lathkill Dale. A gate marks the start of a steeper descent down steps to the wooded base of Cales Dale, where a fingerpost shows the way right to Lathkill Dale.

Once across the footbridge over the River Lathkill, a right turn takes you down the dale for the next 3km of easy walking. After 1km, you pass the pond at Carter's Mill and enter Palmerston Wood. It is well worth taking your time here to explore what there is to see, though the river is prone to run dry in summer months. Don't expect to be on your own in high season as this section of the dale certainly attracts the crowds, and with good reason. At the very least, the plethora of

information boards about the wildlife and the history of mining will slow you down, though the laid path makes for hands-in-pockets strolling.

Lower down, a footbridge recrosses the River Lathkill and allows you to nose around the ruins of Bateman's House, where you can also descend the shaft that lies beneath. A little further on, off to the left, are the ruins of the impressive engine house of Mandale Mine, which used to house machinery to pump water out of the leadmines. At the road and houses at the lower end of Lathkill Dale, you'll need to brace yourself for a left turn back up the steep lane to Over Haddon.

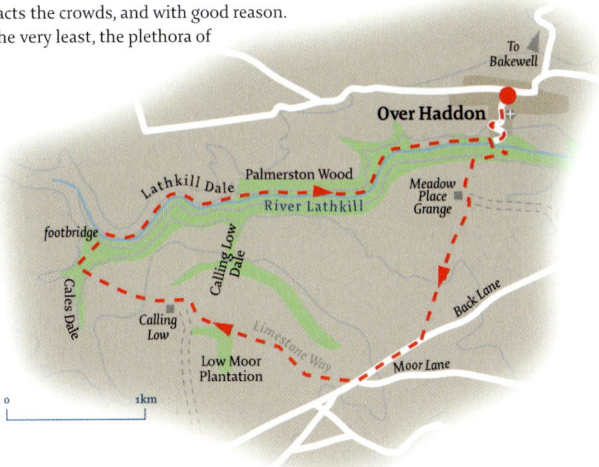

71

Elton and Robin Hood's Stride

Distance 4km **Time** 1 hour 30
Terrain lanes and fields, with some
optional scrambling **Map** OS Explorer
OL24 **Access** bus from Matlock

**Gritstone meets limestone in this short
but varied walk.**

The village of Elton is located 2km west
of Winster and the mix of gritstone and
limestone can be seen in the differing
hues and texture of stone in the houses
and buildings here. The myth of Robin
Hood has been associated with the
natural gritstone outcrop to the north.
The legend is that the rebellious outlaw
jumped between the two pinnacles. Being
always on the run, he was never one for
standing still, but to bridge a 20m gap is

some stride. The outcrop also draws
climbers. The eastern Inaccessible
Pinnacle has a climb called Path of the
Righteous Man. This is perhaps a fitting
nod to the myth of the renegade hero
who personifies fairness and bravery in
the face of corruption and greed. Like the
stride, the climbing route is graded
Extremely Difficult.

From the centre of Elton by the Church
of All Saints walk down Well Street to the
left of the church and in 50m head off left
between houses (SP Youlgreave) to a gate
into fields beyond. Bear left across the top
of the first narrow field, before taking a
sharp right downhill (SP Youlgreave via
Cliff Farm) to the valley bottom, with
good views ahead to the gritstone knoll of
Anthony Hill. From the dip, make a rising
traverse up to the right over four more
fields to Cliff Lane.

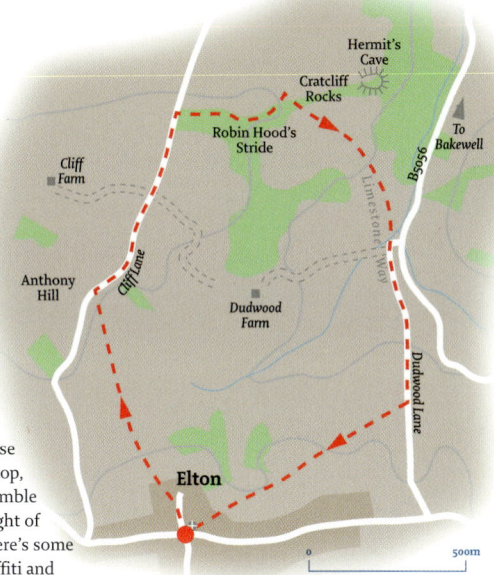

A right turn up the lane for 300m leads past the track to Cliff Farm. You now start to descend and in 250m look out for a path off right along the northern edge of the area of Access Land, which takes you in 200m to the gritstone outcrops of Robin Hood's Stride. For those wanting to reach the top, a straightforward scramble leads up just to the right of the first tor, where there's some considerable rock graffiti and impressive views to delay you.

The route continues around the north side of the rocks to a stile and junction with the Limestone Way. Turn right down the walled track along this waymarked route. In 50m you can detour off to the left over a field to Cratcliff Rocks. A path forks down to the right to some climbing routes and a former hermit's cave near the base of the rocks, though its entrance between two yew trees is now barred by a stone wall and iron railings. Ahead, another straightforward scramble leads up to the top of the rocks for more fine views. Be aware that the drops here are sheer and considerable.

To continue, keep on following the Limestone Way which heads over a field and down a track to the start of Dudwood Lane before ascending this old portway for 500m, steeply up past houses and a stone barn. In another 50m look out on the right for a footpath off the Limestone Way into fields. This path heads up over three fields, veering to the left in the third and over the brow to a wooden pylon. Now descend to a stone stile into the next field and across the top of a small valley, before a fifth field leads you back to the houses on the edge of Elton. Here the path passes between the houses and through the churchyard to bring you back to the start.

◀ The eastern pinnacle of Robin Hood's Stride

73

Matlock and Bonsall

Distance 7km **Time** 2 hours 15
Terrain fields, lanes and woodland paths,
with climbs in and out of Matlock and
Bonsall **Map** OS Explorer OL24
Access train station at Matlock; bus from
Bakewell, Chesterfield and Ashbourne

**Enjoy an over-and-down-dale route from
the popular town of Matlock.**

Matlock lies to the southeast of the
national park and outside its actual
boundary. The town used to be known by
the collective name of The Matlocks,
owing to the string of places along the
Derwent Valley – Matlock Bank, Matlock
Town, Matlock Bridge, Matlock Dale and
Matlock Bath. This last hints at the spa
establishments erected from the 18th
century to exploit the warm springs in
the limestone gorge, with a further spa
centre up the valley at Matlock Bank.
People still flock to the town and many

are uplifted by the cable-car ride to the
Heights of Abraham, but this route takes
you there by climbing the plateau to the
south and circling round via the backdoor
of Bonsall, an attractive hillside village
whose houses are built of an almost
white limestone.

The walk starts from Crown Square in
the centre of Matlock, near the railway and
bus stations. Walk across the roadbridge
over the River Derwent and cross the busy
main road. The first part of the route
follows the Limestone Way as it heads up
Snitterton Road for 50m and bears left
over the railway to Bridge Farm and the
fields beyond.

The route now heads uphill for the next
2km, but with increasingly good views. Go
straight up the steep first field, across a
lane and along the bottom of the second
field into a third. Now follow the field-
edges over the next seven fields up to

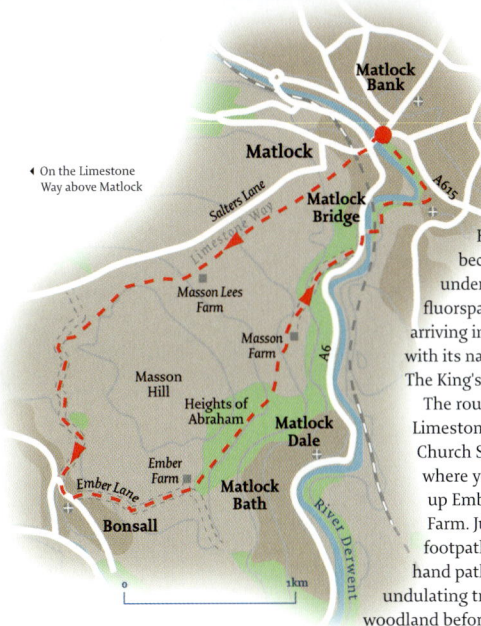

◀ On the Limestone Way above Matlock

then continues on a steepening descent. For the last section it becomes a concrete track underfoot, a relic of the fluorspar workings on Masson Hill, arriving in the village of Bonsall, with its narrow lanes and two pubs, The King's Head and the Barley Mow.

The route now leaves the Limestone Way and heads left up Church Street to St James' Church, where you should turn left steeply up Ember Lane to Ember Lane Farm. Just beyond, at the footpath junction, take the left-hand path to Matlock. This undulating trail heads through woodland before descending to the Heights of Abraham top station. Here, pick up signs for the Derwent Valley Walk (DVW) and keep descending through scrub woodland and fields to pass to the left of Masson Farm. Continue through woodland to join a lane which takes you down to the A6 main road.

A dogleg left for 5m, then right across the road leads to a footbridge over the River Derwent, beyond which you should turn left with the DVW onto the riverside walkway. This takes you round the cliff of Pic Tor, past the former Ladygate Mine and on to Knowlestone Pumping Station. Here the DVW turns left over a footbridge, and left again into Hall Leys Park for 400m back to Crown Square.

Masson Lees Farm. Keeping to the right of the farm, the Limestone Way climbs the next two fields to a track, where it doglegs right for 30m, then left to continue up two more fields. Here the route levels out, crossing through the wall on the right and heading over another field and a second track. Two final fields take you between stone barns, where you should bear to the right to reach a gate onto an old lane.

A left turn onto this delightful lane soon has you twisting your way downhill. After 200m, at a gate, carry on down into woodland. At this point the Limestone Way bears right for 50m before veering back to the left between stone walls and

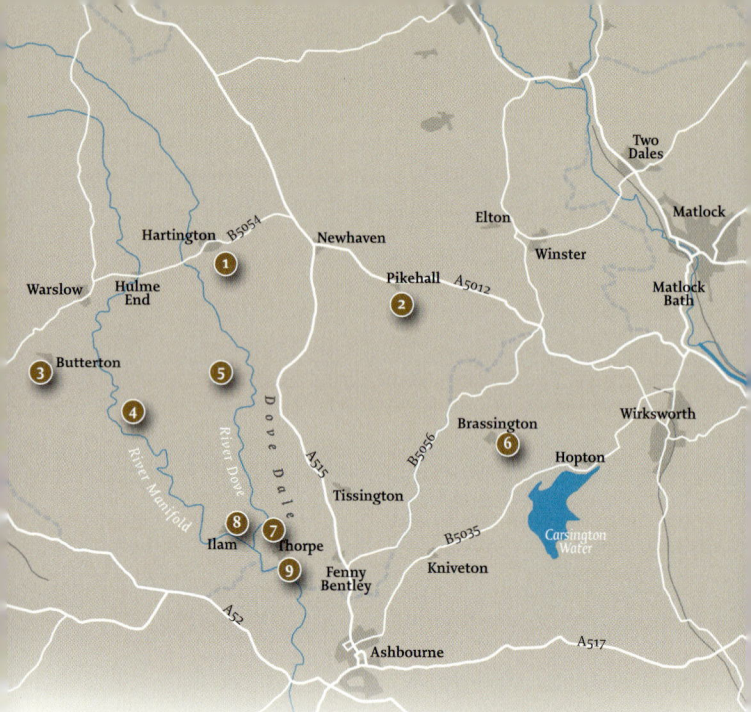

The Derbyshire market town of Ashbourne stands at what many take as the southern edge of the Peak District. Running north from the town is the A515 and on either side are found some of the best known places in the Peak. To the west of the road lies the most famous dale of all, Dovedale. Its picturesque scenery of woodlands and limestone cliffs have long drawn innumerable crowds, but it's no less impressive even now when the steep-sided flanks of Bunster Hill and Thorpe Cloud are sighted.

Just to the west runs the River Manifold, which flows down from the hills of the Upper Dove, past Wetton Hill and Thor's Cave, to Ilam and its confluence with the Dove. Further west still is the enclosing high ground of Grindon Moor, as gritstone once again overtops the limestone. Back across the A515 to the east is the more expansive and open landscape running from Minninglow Hill down to Harboro' Rocks above Carsington Water, a reservoir only 30 years old and, unlike its cousins in the Dark Peak, fed by rivers running through limestone and so rich in wildlife.

Ashbourne and the South

Hartington Three Dale Loop

Distance 9.5km **Time** 2 hours 30
Terrain lanes, tracks and fields with one
moderate ascent out of Hartington
Map OS Explorer OL24 **Access** bus from
Ashbourne and Buxton

**A hands-in-pockets walk of contrasts
from the high ground above Hartington
to the enclosed depths of two of the
Peak's best-known dales.**

Hartington is an attractive village with
its shops and cafés. It was once known for
its Stilton, amongst other cheeses, and
some still come for this – production
temporarily stopped after the closure of
Dove Dairy in 2009, but a small new
venture was set up a few years after this
and the tradition continues. While here it
is also worth a visit to the parish church,
dedicated to St Giles, guardian of an
impressive eight churches in the area. His
name is perhaps not as widely known as

some, but in the 8th century his cult
spread from Provence where he had lived
as a hermit with his hind that he had
rescued from hunters.

From the war memorial in the centre of
Hartington, head up Hall Bank past the
entrance to the youth hostel and, just
before a stone barn in another 150m, turn
right onto Highfield Lane. This delightful
walled lane rises gently uphill for the next
1km past a renovated stone barn and over
the high point, with good views to
Wolfscote Hill, before descending to the
road at the head of Biggin Dale.

A right turn along the road for 75m
takes you round the bend, where you can
bear right onto a footpath which heads
down into Biggin Dale itself. The grassy
way soon narrows as the sides of the dale
close in and become steeper and, after
1km, the route circles round a small pond
before bearing to the right. The dale now

◄ In Wolfscote Dale

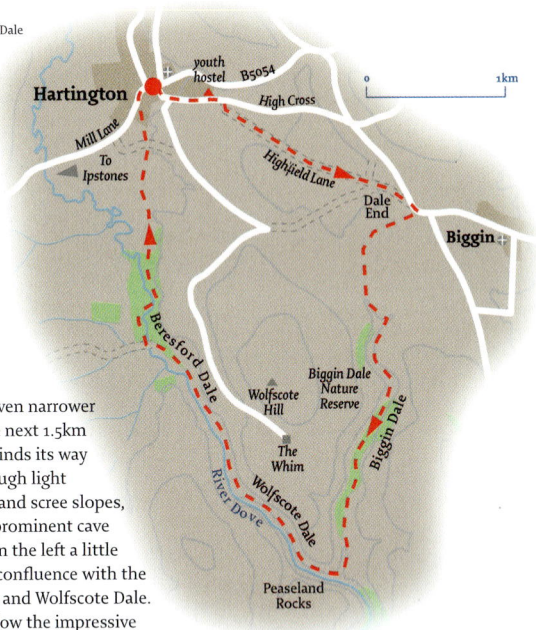

becomes even narrower
and for the next 1.5km
the path winds its way
down through light
woodland and scree slopes,
passing a prominent cave
entrance on the left a little
above the confluence with the
River Dove and Wolfscote Dale.

Here, below the impressive
limestone crags of Peaseland Rocks,
where peregrines are known to nest, turn
right and follow the laid path upstream
beside the river for the next 2km of easy
walking to the grassy top end of the dale,
where the terrain opens out a little and
there are a number of caves in the cliffs
up to the right.

The route now heads over a field, with
the River Dove away to the left, before
doglegging left, then right over a
footbridge (SP Hartington) to continue

on the opposite bank up the enclosed
and wooded Beresford Dale. In 250m the
path switches banks once more and in
another 200m it rises away from the river
to the edge of the woodland and into the
fields beyond.

From here, waymarks show you the
route as the clear path snakes its way
over the grassy fields for 700m before
crossing over a green lane and reaching
Mill Lane, just down from the centre
of Hartington.

Minninglow Hill and Roystone Grange

Distance 5.5km **Time** 1 hour 30
Terrain graded trail, field paths, tracks
and lanes **Map** OS Explorer OL24
Access no public transport to the start

**This is an easy walk, full of history and
great if you want to take things slowly.**

The walk starts 1km south of Pikehall,
on the A5012, at Minninglow car park, a
former railway goods yard on what is now
the Pennine Bridleway and High Peak
Trail (HPT). This follows the old line of
The Cromford and High Peak Railway,
one of the first railways in the world.
It extended 53km and was built between
1825 and 1830 to link the Peak Forest Canal
at Whaley Bridge to the Cromford Canal.
The railway itself was designed like a
canal and on the flat sections the wagons
were pulled by horses, while cables
powered by steam beam engines pulled
the wagons up the steep inclines.

Follow the HPT eastwards out of the
back of the car park, across a lane and
along the impressive embankment.
At busy times you'll be sharing this with
other walkers, horse riders and cyclists,
and there are some impressive views.
The track soon curves to the right and
for the next 1km makes a beeline for
Minninglow Hill, topped on the horizon
with its stand of trees. After passing
through a cutting of rock you reach
Minninglow Quarry, a sheltered spot
for a picnic.

Just beyond, you should bear left off the
HPT and onto a permissive path over
fields up through old walls and limestone
outcrops to the tree-ringed top of
Minninglow Hill, with its ancient tumuli
and stone slabs dating from the Neolithic

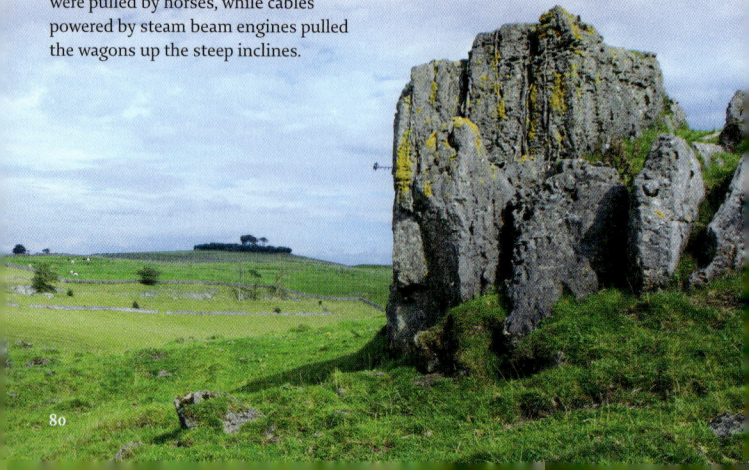

period and the Bronze Age. Excavations in the 19th century found the chambers to contain human bones, including one skeleton, fragments of Romano-British pottery and a number of Roman coins.

The permissive path makes for a gate on the far side, where it bears half-right down two fields to Gallowlow Lane. A footpath continues over the next field, before passing under a former railway bridge of the HPT and heading down two more fields, where you should switch onto a track on the left side of the field-wall. The track takes you down another

two fields, where the footpath bears off to the right and up to a byway, just south of Roystone Grange. Here, you can detour left to a Victorian pumphouse and the site of the former Roystone Grange, which from the 12th to the 14th century was a monastic sheep farm.

The onward route heads right up the byway track and through the current buildings of Roystone Grange, passing the site on the left of a former Roman farmstead just above the modern farm, and along the meandering track below Roystone Rocks – these lie in Access Land and give a good view over the surrounding area. After another 500m the track rises past Roystone Cottages to a junction with Minninglow Lane. Here, bear left up to a road junction, where a right turn (signposted for Minninglow car park) takes you along the tree-lined road for 500m back to the start.

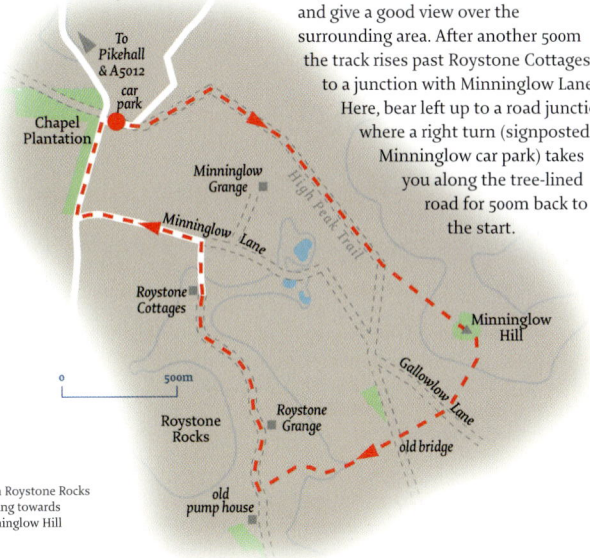

◀ From Roystone Rocks looking towards Minninglow Hill

81

Grindon Moor

Distance 8.5km **Time** 2 hours 30
Terrain lanes and fields with two climbs;
some sections can be wet underfoot
Map OS Explorer OL24 **Access** no public
transport to the start

**If you want to get away from the crowds,
you'll appreciate Grindon Moor and the
villages on the higher ground to the west
of the Manifold Gorge.**

From the centre of the village of
Butterton head down Church Lane past
the Black Lion Inn and down the
Causeway to the ford over the Hoo Brook.
Continue up the road on the other side
for 75m and take the footpath off right
between some cottages before bearing
left into fields at the rear. There is now a
steady climb up the right-hand edges of

a series of five fields with good views
back to the north. In the fifth field bear
slightly right to reach the road running
along the top of Grindon Moor and
some panoramic views.

A dogleg right for 30m along the road,
then left takes you into fields above the
Hamps Valley. Make for the left of the
buildings of Sheldon Farm and then, 50m
beyond, switch to the right side of the
wall and head down a series of fields. In
the fourth field you pick up a track, which
can be muddy, to some farm buildings.
Once through the farmyard you should
keep to the right to head through a gate
to the road in the village of Ford.

The route now turns right through the
village and across the bridge over the
River Hamps. Here, turn right along

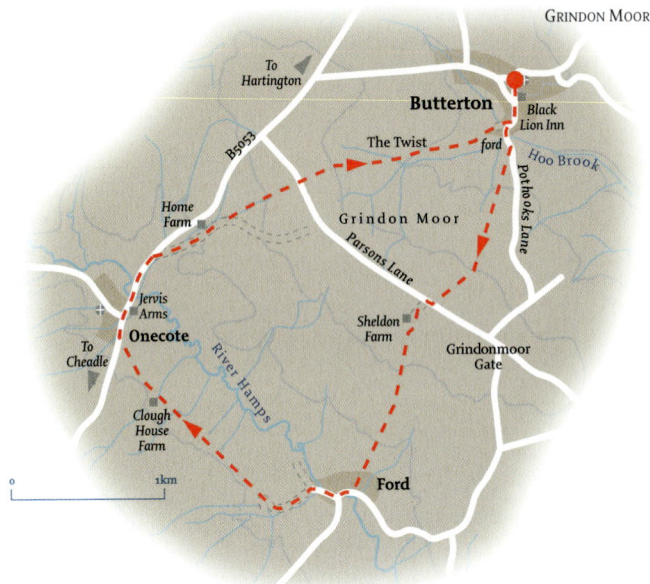

Wetley Lane which follows the other side of the river before starting to rise past cottages. After 200m, where the lane bends sharply to the left, keep ahead onto a footpath into fields. The grassy field-edge track rises steadily to a high point. Beyond, the path makes its way along an old overgrown walled lane, past a ruin, to reach Clough House Farm. Keep along the farm lane, whose surface soon becomes metalled, to the B5053. Here, a right turn takes you down into Onecote, with its church dedicated to St Luke and its pub, the Jervis Arms.

To continue, head along the B5053 for 500m and take the narrow lane off right to Home Farm. The lane rises steeply past the farm and after another 150m, where

the lane bends right, look out for the footpath off left into fields. The path continues to climb up past a ruin and across an area of Access Land to bring you once more to the road at the top of Grindon Moor.

Across the road, the footpath continues initially alongside a track, before passing some corrugated barns and heading down a long field to a ruin at the bottom. Here, cross the stream and the bottom of a small field below a house to reach the area called The Twist. The route now heads across these 12 small fields to a final larger field just above houses. About halfway down, bear right onto a narrow walled lane which takes you down once more to the ford at the lower end of Butterton.

◄ The village of Butterton

Wetton Hill and Thor's Cave

Distance 5km **Time** 2 hours
Terrain lanes, grassy slopes and byways;
the slopes of Wetton Hill are steep in
places **Map** OS Explorer OL24
Access no public transport to the start

A hill, a gorge and one of the Peak's
best-known caves make for a short but
energetic route.

The impressive Thor's Cave is on most
visitors' list of places to visit. This
approach starts from the higher ground of
Wetton before descending to the hamlet
of Wettonmill and then following the
former route of the narrow gauge Leek
and Manifold Light Railway, which for 30
years at the start of the 20th century
carried supplies and tourists up and down
the valley, though it is now the preserve
of walkers and cyclists.

From the centre of the village of Wetton
by Ye Olde Royal Oak pub walk up to the
bend above St Margaret's Church and take
the footpath ahead, signed for Back of
Ecton, along the lane. It is worth pausing
to visit the church and to look at Samuel
Carrington's grave, a long-standing local
schoolmaster and archaeologist who
excavated a number of mainly Romano-
British sites in the area. Ignore the
footpath off to the right and head up past
some cottages and a reservoir to a small
quarry beyond. Where the now rough lane
bends left, take the footpath ahead into
Access Land. The path climbs uphill and
then contours round the grassy left flank
of the slope ahead, before heading
diagonally down across a field to a stile in
the wall at the bottom.

Across the stile, turn left over the wall

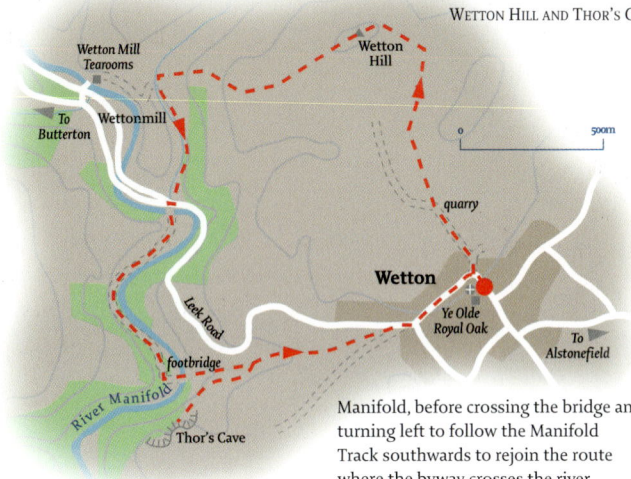

and ascend the grassy eastern slopes of Wetton Hill. Head westwards to the hill's western top for some good views over the Manifold Valley, including Thor's Cave crag. To descend from this point you should initially head WNW and some care is needed down the hill's western side to reach the byway running along the bottom, but in good conditions the steep grassy slopes hold no difficulty, though you should avoid straying to the left. (For an alternative and easier descent, retrace the ascent route and then turn left to follow the path alongside a wall northwards down to the byway along the hill's northern edge to Wettonmill.)

At the byway at the bottom of the western slopes it's worth a detour to the National Trust buildings and Wetton Mill Tearoom – cross the byway and head up the bridleway, over the rise and down to the tearoom and buildings by the River

Manifold, before crossing the bridge and turning left to follow the Manifold Track southwards to rejoin the route where the byway crosses the river.

To continue along the byway after descending Wetton Hill, turn left along the grassy track for 400m to reach the road and the River Manifold, where you should join the Manifold Track from Wettonmill. Follow this riverside track for 600m to a footbridge back over the course of the river. The river, unless the water table is high, has the habit of disappearing down sinks in the riverbed. The route now heads up through woodland for 150m, at which point you can detour off right along a laid side-path to Thor's Cave. The cave itself was formed when the river occupied a far higher level than it currently does, and underground streams flowing below the floor of the river cut out the cave.

To continue, return to the main path and keep on uphill to the top of the wood. From here, the path heads up two fields to the houses of Wetton.

◀ On Wetton Hill looking down the Manifold Valley to Thor's Cave

Alstonefield and Shining Tor

Distance 6km **Time** 2 hours
Terrain lanes, fields and tracks with
two descents and ascents
Map OS Explorer OL24 **Access** no public
transport to the start

**Dramatic views and scenery accompany
you all the way, though you'll need
plenty of strength in the legs for the ups
and downs.**

Alstonefield is a pretty village on the
limestone plateau between Dove Dale to
the east and the Manifold Valley to the
west. From the green in the centre of the
village head eastwards along the road for
400m towards Lode Mill and Ashbourne.
Take the bridleway off left along a walled
track (SP Coldeaton Bridge). You soon
pass the youth hostel and an old stone
barn, beyond which this pleasant way
narrows as it passes between fields and
descends to Gipsy Bank and the edge of

Access Land. The route now descends
steeper open ground down to Coldeaton
Bridge over the River Dove.

Across the bridge, turn right to follow
the twisting riverside path for the next
1km to the roadbridge at Lode Mill, where
the crag of Shining Tor looms up beyond.
Here, a dogleg left along the road and
then right through a gate takes you onto
a path that runs parallel with the road for
300m past a rocky outcrop, before heading
right more steeply up a grassy side valley.

At the top of the rise at a cross-paths,
take the footpath to Milldale, which
follows the wall along the top of Shining
Tor, an impressive limestone outcrop
(not to be confused with the well-known
hill). You can detour to the right for cliff-
edge views back up Dovedale. The wall
and footpath now bend a little to the left
for the next 500m, before the route
crosses the wall into Access Land and

◂ Viator's Bridge in Milldale

zigzags down into Milldale and the famous Viator's Bridge, which probably dates to the 16th century and is named after one of the characters in Izaak Walton's *The Compleat Angler*, a fictional dialogue between a *Viator* (Izaak Walton) and a *Piscator* (his friend, Charles Cotton).

Across the bridge, you can detour left for the National Trust Information Barn, but the route itself bears right along the lane to a junction, where you should take the middle of the three lanes up past a small cottage shop. In 50m by a postbox and old telephone box, look out for a footpath off left. This narrow way squeezes up between cottages to the fields beyond, where you'll need some reserves of energy for the steep ascent. Turn left up the first field and then make for the top right corner in the second, before heading diagonally across the third and bearing to the right in the fourth to reach Millway Lane. Here, a left turn passes the church, which contains the Cotton family pew, and takes you back to the centre of Alstonefield.

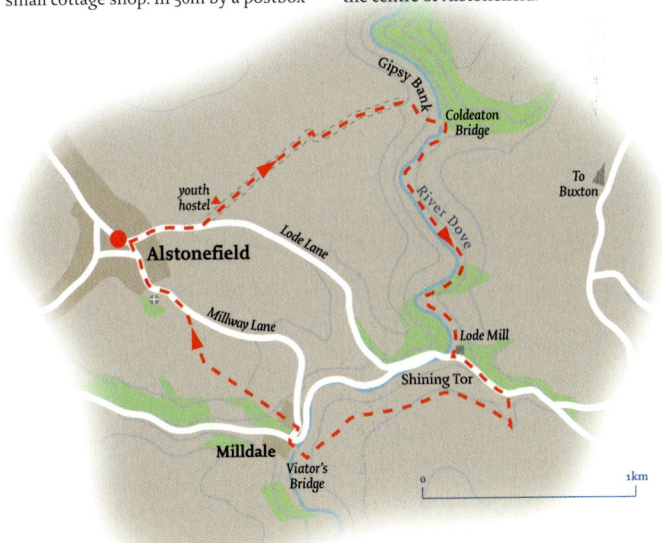

Harboro' Rocks and Carsington Pasture

Distance 7km **Time** 2 hours 15
Terrain lanes, fields and trails with one
steep descent **Map** OS Explorer OL24
Access buses to Brassington from
Ashbourne and Matlock

**Step back in time on a route which takes
in the old mining area of Carsington
Pasture and two former mining villages.**

From the centre of Brassington walk up
Town Street and the road to Longcliffe,
heading north out of the village. Take the
first lane on the right, called Wirksworth
Dale, which heads gently uphill past a car
park and picnic area, a good alternative
starting point in high season. The lane
gives out just before Bee Nest Mine. Here,
turn left onto a footpath for 400m over a
bouldery field along the wall to the right,
kinking right, then left to reach

Manystones Lane. A dogleg right
along the road for 300m leads you past
the mineralworks to a footpath off left
to the High Peak Trail and Harboro' Rocks
beyond. Here you can detour up to the
top of the rocks – initially keep straight
ahead, then make a rising traverse to the
left to reach the triangulation point and
some good views. There is a Neolithic
tomb, and excavations at the start of
the 20th century found pottery and
brooches to indicate people lived here
during the Iron Age.

To continue, head eastwards along the
High Peak Trail for 800m. Just before a
gate, take the footpath off right, across
the road into Carsington Pasture, an area
pockmarked by old leadmines and
limestone quarries. The path follows the
wall on the left down across a dip – the

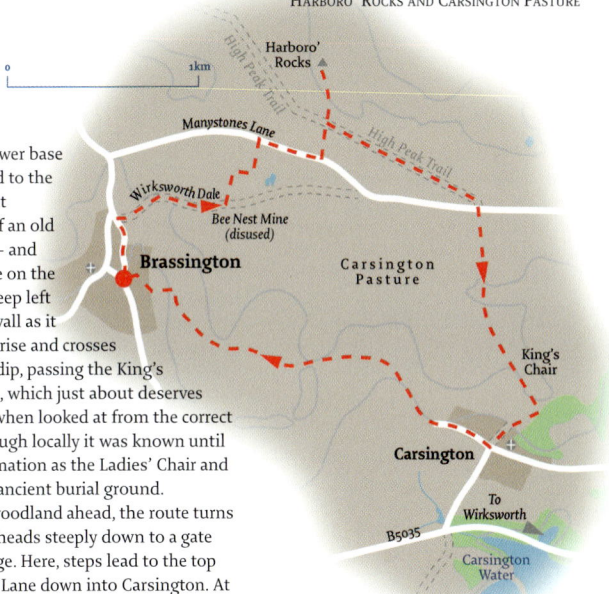

circular tower base in the field to the left is what remains of an old windmill – and up the rise on the far side. Keep left with the wall as it crests the rise and crosses a smaller dip, passing the King's Chair rock, which just about deserves its name when looked at from the correct angle, though locally it was known until the Reformation as the Ladies' Chair and marks an ancient burial ground.

At the woodland ahead, the route turns right and heads steeply down to a gate by a cottage. Here, steps lead to the top of Mining Lane down into Carsington. At the bottom of the lane by the crossroads, you can detour left into the village. The Church of St Margaret has some interesting features and associations, not least the modern stained-glass which depicts a centurion carrying an urn, a reference both to an archaeological find at the end of the 18th century of a Roman funerary urn bearing an abbreviated inscription to 'Gellius, Prefect of the Third Cohort of the Sixth Legion Victorius in Britain' and to the local Gell family's possible origins in ancient Rome.

To continue, turn right at the crossroads past the houses, beyond which a footpath continues along the southern edge of Carsington Pasture past former mining rakes. After 600m at a stile, where the wall alongside the footpath bends to the left, continue straight on up over the brow of the rise ahead. Keep heading westwards over fields and a dip to a ruin by a track, across which the footpath continues uphill. After 100m make sure you keep on the footpath, which veers a little to the left below an area of mineshafts.

Once over the shoulder of the hill, the footpath starts to descend and curves to the right, contouring alongside a stone wall. After 100m, look out for a stone stile which takes you left across the wall and down three fields back to the lower end of Brassington.

Thorpe Cloud and Bunster Hill

Distance 7km **Time** 2 hours 30
Terrain riverside paths with some very
steep slopes and 450m of ascent, with the
final section of descent requiring a short
scramble **Map** OS Explorer OL24
Access no public transport to the start

**This is a mini-mountaineering outing,
where some steep gradients and exposed
terrain require a head for heights.**

Dovedale is one of the most famous
places in the Peak District and its steep
wooded gorge and limestone rocks
forming towers, caves and spires have
attracted visitors for more than 200 years.

The walk starts from Dovedale Car Park.
Follow the walkway upstream alongside
the River Dove for 100m, cross the
footbridge and bear right away
from the river for 100m to a

point where you can turn left up the open
slopes of Thorpe Cloud. The initial climb
is steep but once on the actual west ridge
the going is a little easier to the top, from
where you are treated to panoramic views.
The descent starts a little to the west of
the high point and takes you down the
hill's steep north ridge, from which you
can size up the final scramble required
down Bunster Hill across the river at the
end of the route.

Back down in Dovedale, turn right with
the crowds up the well-trodden riverside
path for the next 2.5km as you pass the
well-known craggy landmarks of Lover's

Leap, the Twelve Apostles, Tissington Spires and Pickering Tor. The path broadens out as it nears Ilam Rock and a footbridge allows you to cross to the far bank.

Here, veer left around the base of Ilam Rock and head up to its left on a steep path into woodland. The gradient soon eases and the path heads slightly right, before steepening once more on its way up to join a footpath running along the top of the dale. A left turn leads you along the top edge of Dovedale Wood for 350m to reach a gate.

The footpath now heads slightly downhill into fields and passes below Air Cottage, before circling right on a well-waymarked section up to a track which takes you to Ilamtops Farm. At the farm gateway, turn left with the track up to a stone barn and continue over the felltop field beyond, following the wall on the right.

Here, a gate leads you into the Access Land of Bunster Hill. Keep left along the wall for 250m and then bear sharp left with the wall, down across the dip ahead, with the actual top of Bunster Hill inaccessible up to the left. After the second stile-crossing, veer right over the rocky knolls of the hill's eastern ridge. At first the descent is gentle. Keep on the crest and, as the gradient steepens lower down, avoid dropping down to the right onto very steep ground but keep to the left to reach the ridge's prominent final knoll. Here, zigzag to the right before heading back to the left on steeper ground. A final zag to the right brings you to a last challenge – a short scramble down a limestone outcrop, though there is no real difficulty once hand and footholds are located.

Once down, turn right along the lane or cross the stepping stones over the River Dove to the path back to the start.

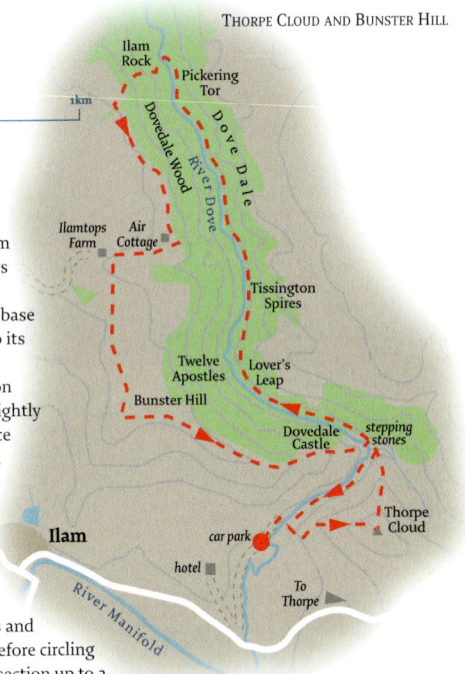

◄ The west ridge of Thorpe Cloud

Ilam and the Manifold Valley

Distance 6km **Time** 2 hours
Terrain lanes, fields and riverside
with 250m of ascent and descent
Map OS Explorer OL24 **Access** no public
transport to the start

A quiet stroll from the village of Ilam
which stands just west of the confluence
of the Manifold and the Dove.

Ilam village and its Hall were
redesigned and rebuilt in the 1820s as a
model village at the instigation of the
wealthy businessman and member of
parliament Jesse Watts Russell. He also

erected Ilam Cross in memory of his wife
Mary. This Gothic Revival memorial has
recently been restored.

The walk starts from the village of Ilam,
where there is limited parking.
Alternatively, the National Trust car park
at Ilam Hall is available. From the centre
of the village head along the road to Blore
past the Watts Russell Memorial and over
the River Manifold. The road rises past the
entrance to Ilam Meadows Farm and
round a bend, where the gradient
increases. Here, look out for a footpath
off left. This heads across fields on a

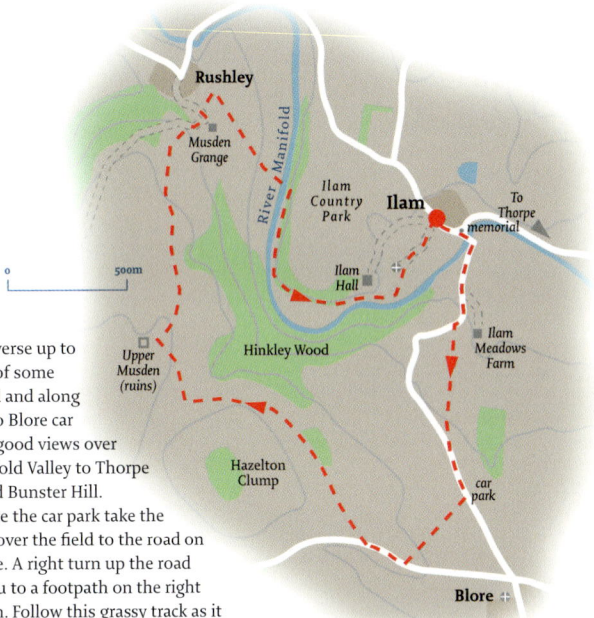

rising traverse up to the edge of some woodland and along its edge to Blore car park and good views over the Manifold Valley to Thorpe Cloud and Bunster Hill.

Opposite the car park take the footpath over the field to the road on its far side. A right turn up the road brings you to a footpath on the right after 100m. Follow this grassy track as it leads over the shoulder of the hill and down across a substantial dip before climbing once more and veering left up to the ruins of the abandoned farmhouse at Upper Musden.

Here, over the wall by the first ruined building, turn sharp right and cross the field to a stone stile, beyond which you should bear left on a descending traverse, in 50m picking up a wall on the left. The path crosses a dip, on the far side becoming more of a track, and in the second dip it veers away from the wall to head down in the direction of Musden Grange. Just above the buildings, as the

path goes through a wall, turn right and follow the wall down past the farm entrance and on down the field beyond.

Now turn right and head over a series of four fields, initially below Musden Grange, before dropping left down to a footbridge over the River Manifold. A right turn onto the pleasant riverside walkway takes you through the parkland of Ilam Hall to the main house, which is managed by the National Trust, and its tearooms. The footpath continues along the main driveway back to the centre of Ilam.

◀ Holy Cross Church, Ilam with Thorpe Cloud beyond

Thorpe and Okeover Park

Distance 10km **Time** 2 hours 30
Terrain lanes, fields and parkland
Map OS Explorer OL24 **Access** no public
transport to the start

An unpretentious village, tree-studded
parkland and riverside paths take you a
world away from nearby Dovedale.

The walk starts from the main car park
500m east of the centre of the village of
Thorpe, opposite the Old Dog pub. Out of
high season it may be possible to park in
the village near the church.

Head along Wintercroft Lane for 400m,
before turning left down Hall Lane. At the
bend bear left along Church Lane, past the
Church of St Leonard, to a gate at the end.
The church has a Norman tower and
inside to the left of the altar the touching
memorial from a father to his 11-year-old
son. From here a track branches to the

right and descends over fields to Coldwall
Bridge and the River Dove. On the far side,
continue on the grassy track as it curves
left up the field and between the
buildings of Coldwall Farm to a lane.

Cross the lane and take the footpath
into the field opposite – a fingerpost
marks the route across the middle of the
field and down to the bottom right
corner. Here, cross a small stream before
heading to the right diagonally up the
next field, where a telegraph pole acts as a
marker, to reach a lane. Turn left past the
houses for just 50m before looking out for
the footpath off left alongside a stone
barn down to an old walled lane. In 150m,
at an old field barn, the path forks. Keep
ahead to a gate into a series of fields
where the path now follows the fence on
the right, with good views to the left. In
the fourth field, pass just below the

former farm of Martin Hill and, at the stone barn, take the footpath off left alongside a wall and into the open parkland of Okeover Hall.

The waymarked route now passes a small pool before crossing a large field – aim for the gate in the gap between stands of woodland. From here, you pass a ruined house in the second field, before descending down through the tree-dotted park and across the grounds in front of Okeover Hall. Follow the marker posts over the driveway and on for another 100m to reach the road, where a right turn takes you to Okeover Bridge across the River Dove. At this point, you can make a

detour along the road into the village of Mapleton, with its pub, the Okeover Arms, and the unusual Italianate church of St Mary.

To continue, on the far side of Okeover Bridge take the footpath off left into fields. The route hugs the River Dove for the next 1.75km until you reach a gate at the edge of woodland. Here, take the right fork (SP Thorpe) up through the trees and then up three final fields to reach the end of Church Lane once more, from where the outward route can be retraced.

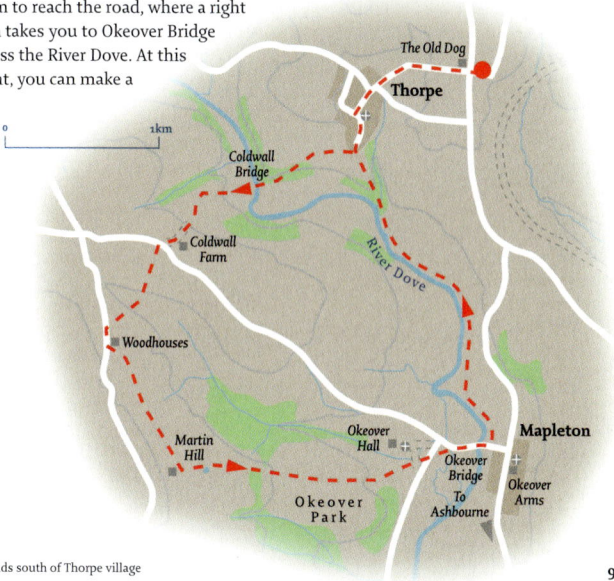

The Old Dog

Thorpe

0   1km

Coldwall
Bridge

Coldwall
Farm

River Dove

Woodhouses

Martin
Hill

Okeover
Hall

Mapleton

Okeover
Bridge

To
Ashbourne

Okeover
Arms

Okeover
Park

◀ Fields south of Thorpe village

Index